TODAY
I WILL NOT
DIE

TODAY
I WILL NOT
 DIE

Dr. Mary Ann Block

TWIN STREAMS
Kensington Publishing Corp.
http://www.kensingtonbooks.com

The recommendations made in this book should be followed in accordance with the advice of your own health care practitioner. If you are undergoing medical treatment, consult with your physician before making any changes in your medical regimen. The author and publisher are in no way responsible for the efficacy of any products or services mentioned herein.

KENSINGTON BOOKS are published by

Kensington Publishing Corp.
850 Third Avenue
New York, NY 10022

All Kensington titles, imprints and distributed lines are available at special quantity discounts for bulk purchases for sales promotion, premiums, fund raising, educational or institutional use.

Special book excerpts or customized printings can also be created to fit specific needs. For details, write or phone the office of the Kensington Special Sales Manager: Kensington Publishing Corp., 850 Third Avenue, New York, NY, 10022, Attn. Special Sales Department. Phone: 1-800-221-2647.

Kensington and the K logo Reg. U.S. Pat. & TM Off.
Twin Streams and the TS logo are trademarks of the Kensington Publishing Corp.

ISBN 1-57566-708-8

First Kensington Trade Paperback Printing: March, 2001
10 9 8 7 6 5 4 3 2 1

Printed in the United States of America

In Memory of Mimi
In Honor of Mother
The two most courageous women I know

*"We never know the love of our parents for us until
we have become parents."*
—Henry Ward Beecher

Special thanks to:
Alex, Ashley, Bill, Doug, Gary, George, Greg,
Harold, Howard, Ian and Rich
For Helping Us Create the Reality of Life

CONTENTS

PART TWO: TAKING ACTION

PREFACE

My mother raised and infused me with the same philosophy her mother, Mimi, had taught her: "You do whatever you have to do for your children."

I grew up in a home where this was the dominant philosophy. When I got married and had children, this philosophy carried into my own life. However, when my first baby, Michelle, was two years old, she developed a chronic medical problem. To help my daughter get well, I placed my trust in the conventional medical profession. The doctors, including the specialists, not only misdiagnosed her illness, they prescribed a variety of drugs that induced side effects that were potentially life-threatening. Instead of getting better, my daughter's health continued to deteriorate. After going from doctor to doctor who made mistake after mistake with her medications, it became disturbingly clear to me that under the care of her doctors my little girl was becoming gravely ill.

Agonizing years of frustration went by and my daughter's health got progressively worse. Instead of support, the doctors who had been prescribing the drugs had summarily turned their backs on her. Adding insult to injury, one specialist said: "It's all in her head." I was furious. Did this doctor really think my baby girl was a prodigy when it came to hypochondria? As fate would have it, I eventually connected with a fine osteopathic physician who helped me turn the tide toward my daughter's recovery and restored my confidence in medicine.

Still, I was wary of what I didn't know. Out of an inner necessity to make sure my daughter became completely well and remained in good health, I rerouted my anger and frustration into a bold plan. After being a homemaker for 15 years, I entered medical school at the age of thirty-nine. I was apprehensive at first. I could feel my fears poking and prodding me, looking for weakness. How would I fare in medical school at my age? Did I have what it took to make the grade? But fear ultimately struck out. I decided that nothing like the ordeal I had suffered through with my daughter would ever happen to someone I loved again. In my mind, becoming a doctor to protect my family was absolutely necessary. I believed I was doing what any parent would do under the circumstances. I believed in myself.

Seven years after my life-altering decision to become a doctor, I proudly hung out my shingle to practice medicine in my hometown of Fort Worth, Texas. I was elated. My thrill of victory, however, was short-lived. Just as I was starting my private practice, I learned my mother had inoperable, metastatic and terminal lung cancer. Her doctors predicted she had two months to live. Fortunately, I had learned a valuable lesson during my daughter's illness. Doctors don't have all the answers. I would not sit by idly and blindly. I would not accept the prognosis of my mother's demise. I knew doctors can be wrong.

My mother's words were in my head. Yes, I thought, you do whatever is necessary to help your children. By following Mother's nurturing wisdom and caring for my daughter, little did I, or my mother, know that her philosophy would come full circle. I then did what any daughter would do to save her mother. My mother had taught me well.

There's more to this story of how I helped my mother beat the odds and survive terminal lung cancer. I could list what I did as if it were a prescription, a straightforward protocol—see

Part Two of this book. If I did just that, you'd have conclusions but not the understanding of what made this story about healing a success. It would be like me telling you "the butler did it" about a mystery novel that you hadn't read. Revealing the identity of the culprit would have little meaning or impact. You can't separate the cure from the patient. Cures and protocols are like recipes. You can list all the ingredients of a recipe in the precise amounts and how to combine them without achieving the dish as prepared by a master chef. That's why there's an art to cooking. That's why there's an art to healing.

Like the connections among parents, children, uncles, aunts, cousins, and friends, the chain of events that add up to an individual life are inextricably related in a complex web of details, decisions, and the luck of the draw. To be fully appreciated and of practical value, everything must be viewed within a context. It is the thread of love that warmly binds us together in this vast universe. My mother raised me well. Her mother, Mimi, had taught her the rules of life. I was fortunate to have them both.

DR. MARY ANN BLOCK

FOREWORD

There are many lessons we learn in life. None, however, are as important as when we are faced with almost certain death. Such desperate hours provide us with an opportunity to acquire remarkable insights about ourselves. Our lives are not directed by others. We can choose our own directions, our own beliefs, and our own futures. We decide our own reality and our own truths.

Reading this book about Cecile Ritzwoller's journey from terminal cancer to the realm of "cancer-free," we revel in her story of the healthy life she has lived these past nine years despite the mere months she had been given to live by her doctors. Truly, Cecile can say that reports of her death had been greatly exaggerated. Awakened by Cecile's victory, we are motivated to take back ownership of our thoughts, dreams, values, and ultimately our lives.

Cecile's story gives substance to the old adage, "What goes around comes around." The lessons in life that Cecile gave to her daughter returned to her with more power, more love, and more perseverance than she could ever have imagined.

Life's challenges and triumphs unleash incredible strengths and beautiful gifts. The underlying current of this book involves the course of three women, connected forever through time as you will find out. The legacy of how to see the world from Mimi, Cecile's mother, sets the dynamics of the story into motion.

Cecile's daunting duel with cancer and the values she had instilled in her daughter, Mary Ann, will touch you, enlighten you, and hopefully inspire you to face whatever crisis you encounter in your life with the strength and wisdom that is inside of you.

It certainly has for me.

JOAN ANDERSON

PART ONE

MIMI AND CECILE

Chapter 1

❧

Wedding Belles

"I am an optimist. It does not seem too much use being anything else." —Winston Churchill

July 14, 1996

The late afternoon sultry summer sky of Texas was smiling upon us. I looked around, taking in a panorama of colors and people whirling into a joyous blur. I pinched myself. This was my Midsummer Night's Dream. Not only was my darling daughter, Michelle, getting married, my 80-year-old mother, Cecile, was soaking up every delicious moment of her granddaughter's wedding. My 90-year-old father, David Ritzwoller, stood proud, alert, and dapper. Daddy, a quiet, brilliant man with a mind like a computer and a dry sense of humor, was still very much in love with his "Cele." My mother is an outgoing, take-charge individual and the ideal counterpart for my laid-back father. Miraculously, my parents had just celebrated their 59th wedding anniversary the weekend before. When asked the secret of their longevity as a married couple, Daddy quipped, "I let her handle the TV remote."

A perfectly ordinary scene, for all its special feelings. Yet I couldn't believe my eyes.

After being diagnosed with inoperable metastatic terminal

lung cancer five years earlier and given only months to get her "affairs in order" by the medical establishment, my mother was here, today, alive and kicking, and "cancer free." Rubbing elbows with nearly 200 guests at the Colonial Country Club in Fort Worth, my mother was living proof that doctors don't know everything—a fact I had come to learn over the years as both a mother and a physician.

The fine mix of family and friends had arrived to celebrate and embrace the marriage of my precious Michelle to Reggie Goldsmith, a wonderful young man. The pianist filled the chapel with superb entrance music, each note a powerful vibration that sent chills of excitement through my body. Cele, escorted by my 24-year-old son, Randy, proudly walked down the aisle as "grandmother of the bride." As Mother, coifed just so in her natural gray and wearing a fashionable black dress, made her way toward the marriage altar arm-in-arm with Randy, heads turned. Maybe it was the palpable magic in the air that heightened my senses. From a distance, I could distinctly hear people observing how young and wonderful my mother looked. I was exhilarated.

As *Here Comes the Bride* got everyone's attention, Michelle made her entrance, glowing in her exquisite off-the-shoulder white wedding gown. Stan, her father, escorted his daughter toward a bright new future. In the soulful metaphorical center of this celebration of life and renewal was my mother. She laughed and was radiant, ready to live it up at her granddaughter's glorious wedding soiree.

Despite the large company, the sit-down dinner affair felt intimate. The guests were people of good cheer who mingled well. Michelle's dad and I were divorced and Reggie's parents had been divorced as well. Both former and present significant others were getting along. For example, Stan's new wife and I had worked closely on Michelle's wedding plans. Stan and I had always put our children first and his new wife, Cathy, had no problem doing the same. Everyone involved wanted only one thing from this day: a beautiful and perfect wedding for Michelle and Reggie. As the reception that followed swung into gear, I thought of the charmed marriage my parents enjoyed. I sensed Michelle's wedding was charmed as well. Somehow, I was sure of it.

A wedding doesn't just happen. It's a major enterprise, emotionally and strategically. Mother helped out with all her granddaughters' weddings; she wasn't simply a guest who showed up. But it wasn't until Michelle's, in our home town of Fort Worth, rather than in Houston where my nieces lived, that my mother was able to throw herself full throttle into arranging all the details. Since I was busy building up my new practice as a physician, Mother did much of the hard work that came with the territory of planning a wedding. I couldn't have done it without her.

Mother took charge. She had always excelled at organizing things and embraced the particulars of the wedding with a loving fury. Determined to helping her granddaughter find the perfect wedding dress, Mother accompanied Michelle on bridal shop outings. Being an excellent seamstress herself, she had a keen artistic flair and an eye for quality. Being a fine cook herself, Mother was with us when we sampled meals from various caterers for the dinner menu. She also tasted—more like savored—every cake as a wine connoisseur might sample various vintages for just the right Bordeaux. Tasting cakes was a perk for Mother who had a sweet tooth. She had been denied those goodies while fighting the cancer. Her rigid diet prohibited sugar. Winning can be so sweet.

Mother scrutinized every potential invitation, made suggestions and listened carefully. She was our chief of staff. When Michelle made a decision about this or that, Mother would follow up. Efficiency was the name of her game. She was indispensable. She researched, kept notes, made appointments with photographers, and made the necessary phone calls. She organized accommodations at a local hotel for our out-of-town guests, checked on the reception schedule, double-checked with the chef on the menu, and worked hand-in-hand with the florist. Mother was fine-tuning the affair until everything was on key. Not one single thing went wrong. Everything worked beautifully and on cue. Michelle's wedding was perfect.

The music at the Colonial Country Club played well into the evening. Everyone danced and visited. Daddy, looking handsome as ever, tripped the light fantastic with Cele, the bride, and each of his granddaughters throughout the evening. At midnight, the bride and groom escaped all the well-wishers under a loving barrage of birdseed. Mother was there to see the happy couple off—a moment forever etched in my mind's eye. When the wedding was over, Daddy drove Mother home. My parents looked like kids who had been out on a date. It was truly priceless having them with me on the day our family expanded and a new generation was launched. Heritage, accomplishment, self-discovery, and a loving family are what life is all about.

The lights of the country club faded into the distance behind me as I went home that night, flying on the wings of dreams that come true. As I was getting ready for bed, the phone rang. It was one o'clock in the morning. Mother, her voice weak and weary by now, was calling to reminisce about the wedding. I could tell she wanted to relish every moment of the evening we had just shared. After Mother got her fill of the celebration highlights, we said good night.

I sat down on my bed feeling simultaneously exhausted and wide awake. It had been a grand and delicious day. I began fingering the precious wedding band I wore. No, it wasn't the ring my former husband had given me. I rubbed the band my grandmother, Mimi, Cele's mom, had given me as a keepsake more than 20 years ago. Like a magic lamp, the old gold band summoned a special presence that had been with me from my earliest memories. I knew Mimi was in my heart and in my room. She is with me always.

Chapter 2

My Grandmother Mimi

"The past is the present, isn't it? It's the future too."
—Eugene O'Neill

This story begins with my loving, wise, grandmother Mimi who, without my being aware of it at the time, had planted valuable seeds in my head. In the years that followed and just when I would need them most, Mimi's seeds would sprout beautiful thoughts, flowering insights, and the courage to act on my feelings. If it weren't for my brave grandmother, I'm certain my mother wouldn't have lived to see the joy of my daughter's wedding, or the birth of her great-granddaughter, Paige, in 1999. None of the remarkable things that happened in my life would have been possible without Mimi. She was the only grandparent I knew well. I had only seen Daddy's mother a few times in my life and the grandfathers of the family were already dead when I was born. Mimi was the galvanizing force that held our family together. Her two daughters respected her and that admiration naturally trickled down to her grandchildren. Mimi was the most exceptional person I had ever known.

I Remember Mimi

Her name was Minnie Cohen Friedman. We called her Mimi. She was born in Kansas City, Missouri, on November 13, 1892. When she entered the world, telephones were still a novelty, the airplane had not yet been invented, Benjamin Harrison was the 23rd president of the United States and Van Gogh was an unknown artist whose paintings were considered worthless. As one century was approaching the end of its run, a brave new modern world beckoned on the horizon.

Mimi's family had an entrepreneurial spirit. They had immigrated to the United States from Germany and settled in Missouri, the "Show Me" state, in the mid-1800s. Her mother, Marie, died and her father, Moses, sent Mimi and her two brothers, Louis and Adolph, to live with their Aunt Mary and Uncle Jake in El Reno, Oklahoma. They had a son of their own and were less pleased to be raising two more boys. They favored Mimi, however, and were happy to finally have a girl in their home.

In 1912, Mimi married 24-year-old Will Friedman, who was a cotton broker. The young couple set up housekeeping in Galveston, Texas, where the cotton business action took place. The bride was 20 years old. A good life seemed to lie ahead. But, in 1918, a devastating influenza epidemic swept across the country. Antibiotics had not yet been discovered and millions died during the outbreak, including her husband, who had just turned 29.

Mimi, now 25, was left a widow with two baby girls to raise—my future mother, Cecile, and her older sister, Marie. Mimi knew how to stretch a buck. She lived on the life insurance money her husband had left when he died. Mimi made the money last until Cecile and Marie had grown up. Somehow, she managed the impossible and didn't burden her kids with adult problems.

After her husband had died, Mimi left Galveston for Fort Worth and moved in with her mother-in-law, Hanna Friedman, for a while. Some time later, Mimi and her daughters would move into their own apartment where they were eventually joined by her father and brother, Adolph. By this time, her other brother, Louis, was married and on his own.

Mimi was a doer, especially when it came to keeping her family together. A distant relative, with a retail establishment in Oklahoma City, offered Mimi's older daughter, Marie, a job in the advertising department. Marie was a commercial artist and jumped at the opportunity. Mimi also pulled up stakes in Fort Worth and moved her family northward to a new state where she worked in the ladies' ready-to-wear department of the store owned by the same relative who employed Marie.

Mimi and her daughters were close. They were a family. They learned from necessity to work things out among themselves. Over the course of their lives, they developed a profound bond that helped them cope during hard times. They lived through Will's death, the Great Depression and two world wars. My mother remembers that Mimi had gotten angry at her only once, and that was when she was 16 years old and in high school. She had stayed out until four o'clock in the morning with her friends. Whether Mimi had gotten angry with my mother that one time only or not, isn't important. That my mother can recall only that one incident tells a lot about how they got along.

Over the years, Mimi remained close to Louis and Adolph. Like Mimi, both brothers lived into their eighties. Her family came from the deep end of the gene pool when it came to longevity.

When she was a young woman, Mimi had suitors. She chose

not to remarry, which was unusual in her time. Although she admired a strong, conventional, family unit with a father, mother and children, she weighed the consequences of her decisions as a mother. Mimi did keep company with one particular bachelor for a long time, but ultimately didn't think he'd make a good father. After that romance was over, she went with a much older gentleman; as it turned out their relationship remained in the "good friends" category. Mimi had two girls who needed raising and they couldn't have chosen a better mother. She held them together, especially through the hard times— when families can be ripped apart by circumstances.

Born in the 19th century, Mimi was, for the most part, not shackled with mindless conventions of the past. She was a remarkably independent woman with a positive attitude. Whenever others got bogged down in dogma, she had a wider perspective and always saw an alternative—that was her priceless nature. I'll never know what made her develop and adopt this progressive posture toward life. Losing her own mother at a very young age, raised by an uncle and aunt, and widowed at 25 with two children to raise, were certainly potent life lessons. Mimi survived the hardships that stood in her path. By overcoming obstacles and believing in herself, Mimi built character into her being.

Maybe it was none of the above.

Perhaps Mimi was born with an innate sense of the larger scheme of things in this life, or she was able to tune into a higher wisdom that required a special sensitivity on her part. Whatever the reason, Mimi maintained a healthy self-image. She knew we define our own lives, our own limitations, and our own successes. She was an exceptional individual who advocated from experience that a person could accomplish much with the positive power of thought, and that the effects were cumulative. My Mimi had magic in her soul and I knew it from my earliest memory.

My dear Mimi spoke to me often about life, passing on her wisdom in a tone that said this really mattered. Biologically, I had Mimi's genes stirring within me. Mimi had a "green thumb" and was my gardener in all respects. She began planting those powerful seeds in my head when I was a child and she never stopped—for which I'm eternally grateful. Mimi loved all her grandchildren with an equal passion. She gave us all everything she had to give. Seeds of conviction are delicate and need the right soil and climate to grow. Without knowing it at the time, I was a hothouse for Mimi's seeds.

"Mary Ann," she would say in her gentle manner, holding my hand in hers, her face beaming with kindness, "a person can go a long way toward achieving anything if they put their mind to it. The mind and body are connected in special and powerful ways. Most people don't yet realize this. Remember what I'm telling you and you'll be ahead of the game as you grow up. Oftentimes you can think yourself out of illness and into health. Oftentimes you can think and will yourself out of problems and into solutions. Thought is a powerful force as real as anything else, as real as air—even though you can't see it."

Even though I was just a kid, I could feel that Mimi was telling me something important. We all understand as much as we can in the moment—no more, no less. Experience continues to be the primary teacher and luck favors the prepared mind. In a nutshell, Mimi was teaching me not to be a victim. She told me that you create your own reality within the circumstances that come your way. I didn't fully grasp the impact and value of her advice at the time, but when I got older and faced impossible odds of my own, that phrase, "You create your own reality," became watchwords that guided me and gave me strength.

Certainly, awareness of the mind/body connection had been around for thousands of years and acknowledged by many ancient cultures around the world. Nevertheless, Mimi was a pioneer. What she considered simple common sense was often considered esoteric or just plain weird by others. She was talking about the power of positive thinking and the mind/body connection decades before it was fashionable. Bookstores did not yet stock the endless rows of books we see today on self-help and positive thinking. Considering that Mimi lived through the Great Depression only made her enlightened outlook on life that much more exceptional.

Mimi knew a lot about what really matters and what she knew would shape and sculpt my life in ways I could not imagine or fully appreciate for years to come. She had instilled family values and a sense of purpose in her daughters. I was fortunate to be the daughter of one of her daughters and to grow up in an extended family that had my grandmother, Mimi, as its heart and soul.

Since I was a shy child, it was no surprise that I loved being with my gregarious grandmother. She had a knack for being able to talk to anyone, a talent I found particularly exciting. Being with Mimi brought out the best in people. When she spoke to someone, she was present with her whole being. No one was a stranger to her. She made everyone feel special. That was her gift. "You never know where your next friend will come from," she told me. I'm sure I absorbed this interpersonal skill from her through osmosis. Later in my life, when I became a doctor and a public speaker, I found Mimi's example of sociable dexterity invaluable. She opened my eyes to the world. She was the beginning of my existence.

Who's Got Mimi?

After my mother married my father, David Herman Ritzwoller, they moved to San Antonio, Texas. Mimi stayed with her daughter, Marie, in Oklahoma City. When Marie married

Daddy's cousin, Jack Berger, Mimi lived with them. Mimi seemed to have lived with my aunt Marie and uncle Jack for as long as I could remember. She was always there, helping take care of my cousins, Joan and Susie. Mimi was organized, a first-rate housekeeper and a wonderful cook. She prepared most of the meals and managed the house. Most working parents today can only fantasize about having an angel like her to help out. She always seemed happy and always made time for her grandchildren. She was entirely dedicated to her family. Anyone who had Mimi in their lives was blessed. She was a rare gem.

Eventually, my parents moved back to Oklahoma City where I was born and would be near my beloved Mimi. Then, all too soon, my aunt and uncle moved to Fort Worth, taking Mimi with them. I was envious of my cousins because they had Mimi full time. I adored her. So did they. Perhaps the 200 miles from Oklahoma City to Fort Worth that separated us also connected us. When it came to Mimi, out of sight definitely didn't mean out of mind. Not having her with me daily taught me to appreciate her all the more. Even as a young child, I fondly and distinctly remember the anticipation of waiting for the weekend when my parents, my brother Steve, and I would get in the family car and drive off to my cousins' house in Fort Worth. I loved visiting my grandmother and nothing would stop me. When my family couldn't make the trip, I would often ride the train all by myself to Fort Worth to visit Mimi and my cousins.

Mimi would always talk *to* me, not *at* me. She never patronized. Some of my fondest memories are of sitting on her bed and listening with rapt attention to her stories of another era. My favorite tale was about her pony named Sugar. Mimi would hide sugar cubes in her hand and let the pony find them—hence the name. She was about 8 years old, living with her aunt Marie and uncle Jake in El Reno at the turn of the century, when American Indians still roamed the Oklahoma countryside. One day, when Mimi was out riding Sugar, she came upon a group of

Indians having a powwow around a fire. For some reason, her pony became excited, reared up, and fell over onto the fire. Fortunately, Mimi was thrown clear. While the Indians laughed and pointed at them, Mimi was frightened and worried that her pony had been burned. She took Sugar by the reins and hurried home where she gently patted butter on Sugar's burns. I could hear Mimi's story about Sugar and the Indians over and over.

As I grew older, I never tired of spending time with my grandmother. I could never get enough of her. Even as a teenager growing up in the '60s, when my hormones were pumping and peer pressure to conform was, as always, intense, I would often choose to go shopping with her instead of staying with my friends whose idea of world affairs was that the Beatles had invaded America.

I was a fortunate grandchild to have a rare connection with my grandmother. Two generations removed, she was far enough away from me emotionally to be both my best friend and a parental figure—a tricky balancing act that she pulled off exceptionally well. When I was with Mimi, I felt no sense of her needing to control me or place demands on me. She worked her magic by establishing a bond and by letting me know she was there for me. I was all ears when she had something to say. "Honey," she'd say, "when you grow up into a fine young woman and have kids of your own, they'll watch how you treat your parents. Love and respect your parents, and your kids will follow the lead."

She was one smart lady.

Chapter 3

Thoroughly Modern Mimi

"Of all the rights of woman, the greatest is to be a mother."
—Lin Yu-tang

Every bit a part of the 20th century, Mimi was a child of the 19th century as well. Regardless of her chronological age, she remained flexible and grew with the times. When Mimi was 80 years old, I distinctly remember her telling me that she felt half her age—and she acted it by living in the moment and thriving in the present.

Mimi's thinking wasn't totally progressive. She retained holdover notions from another time that favored other values. When my mother was a young schoolgirl, Mimi instructed her not to make good grades. She actually paid my mother not to make A's. Old ways die hard. Tradition said that if a girl was too smart, she wouldn't be able to "catch" a boyfriend. The theory held that a man didn't want a wife who was smarter than he was. Has anything really changed?

By the time I was growing up, Mimi had come around. She had seen the light about girls and grades. Times and values were slowly changing. Men and women could be equal in the academic arena. Mimi no longer felt that a girl making good grades need have a problem in attracting a beau. The ability to change and incorporate new ideas kept Mimi young. On some male/

female role issues, Mimi remained steadfast. While she encouraged me to do things on my own and let me know that so-and-so "could not hold a candle to me," she also warned me to "Let your husband fix this or that." She thought it was best to let my husband do household activities that were considered to be "man's" work. I should let him put together the children's toys or a piece of furniture that needed assembling. That my husband didn't want to fix this or that, or that I enjoyed doing the fixing was irrelevant. Mimi drew a line in the sand when it came to deciding which chores were male and which were female. Although we were separated by more than half a century, nearly a lifetime for some, our kinship could not have been closer. She had always been a part of my life; she had always been there with me and for me. I could not fathom the thought of life without my wonderful grandmother.

Mimi's Menu: Cooking for Body and Soul

It's no great secret that food is a powerful influence on the body and senses. The novel, *Like Water for Chocolate*, by Laura Esquivel, makes this point delectably pungent. Food can heal, enhance romance, and stir up all kinds of things—both good and bad. Food made with love tastes better and is better for you. My love of cooking and cuisine clearly came from two marvelous cooks—my mother and grandmother. Mimi had a repertoire of special recipes. She delighted in preparing them for the whole family—which included my aunt, uncle and cousins.

Mimi loved frying chicken and hers was the best I ever had. She enjoyed the process of preparing food and that is the key to being a wonderful cook. She derived great satisfaction from cutting up chicken into pieces for frying and eating. She used to say, "I enjoy cutting up chickens so much, I should have been a surgeon." Although we laughed good-naturedly at the prospect, I think there was a part of her that knew she could have been a surgeon. In another era more ripe and open with opportunity for women, I had no doubt she could have been a doctor, or anything else she set her mind to doing. Mimi had chosen to be a wonderful mother, and that's a supreme accomplishment by any standard. For the here and now, I was thankful for her tantalizing finger-licking chicken.

Another specialty she prepared for us was Mimi Pancakes. They were light, thin, and, as I later learned, superb crepes—delicacies worthy of any master dessert chef. Mimi would stand at the stove, make them for us in her favorite skillet, and gently place her "pancakes" on our plates. We eagerly shook powdered sugar over them and stuffed ourselves. They were light, airy, and sweet—in a word, delicious! Her "pancakes" were all the more sweet because she made them for us. Mimi Pancakes were not an everyday occurrence. She'd make them now and then, knowing it was important for us to anticipate the upcoming special treat. She sure knew how to keep us hungry for more. I'm sure that waiting made them taste even better—if that was possible. My brother, Steve, could always put away the most at one sitting, a gustatory honor he thoroughly enjoyed.

It wasn't until years later when I made Mimi Pancakes for my two children that I realized how strenuous it must have been for her, especially during her last years when she was in chronic pain, to stand at the stove putting pancake after pancake on our "empty" plates. To Mimi, we must have looked like fledgling birds, our mouths gaping wide open and chirping for morsels to feed our insatiable appetite. Her cooking for us was pure love and that's why I love cooking, too. Although I now know they're made like crepes, look like crepes, and taste like crepes, they will always be Mimi Pancakes to this grateful granddaughter.

When my daughter, Michelle, got married to Reggie, I gave her a cookbook I had put together. It contained all of Mimi's recipes, as well as some from my mother and her dad's mother, Mary, who was also a wonderful cook. These recipes were so much a part of my life and that of my grandmother that I can't fix any of these dishes today without thinking of her. Most of us have experienced a sensory phenomenon that brings up a memory. We sniff a certain aroma or odor in the air that triggers a specific memory associated with it. I want my children to appreciate the sweet memories of recipes lovingly handed down and lovingly prepared.

Mimi's recipe for fudge was the one recipe that oozed through our fingers. No one could make fudge like Mimi. Following her recipe as written down didn't do the trick. She was a fudge master who was willing to share how it's done. The magic ingredient, however, couldn't be taught. You had to find that out for yourself.

There was a "feel" to beating the fudge. "You've got to feel when it's right with your hands," she'd tell me. "See, I can feel the consistency of the fudge resist against my fingers until it gets to be just the right thickness. You have to be patient to get things right." Like a fine jazz musician, she played it by ear and *knew* when it was right.

Years later, when I became an osteopathic physician, my ability to feel (palpate) the body's structural and fluid makeup was an essential tool for healing patients and restoring normal functioning. As a doctor, I discovered I had the healing touch—a "feel" for healing. Although it took a while from the time Mimi had given me cooking lessons, I was finally making "fudge" the right way—my way. Mimi would have been proud of me.

I loved Mimi so much. I wished things would remain the same. These were happy days. I think we all share a longing for those times when things in our lives seemed to be in balance and all was right with the world. Life doesn't remain frozen in time. Change is inevitable and inevitably we all must confront realities that reflect our own mortality. Life tests us in unexpected ways.

Chapter 4

Reality Hurts

"Some doctors make the same mistake for twenty years and call it clinical experience."   —Dr. Noah D. Fabricant

Mimi was not one to complain. She never went to the doctor for some minor ache or pain. I had never known her to be sick—never! No colds, headaches, stomachaches, nothing. If she was sick now and then, she was adept at keeping it to herself. She never whined or fussed about her health. As I mentioned earlier, Mimi believed a positive state of mind could go a long way toward keeping a person well. Traditional Western medicine, for the most part, dismissed the mind/body collaboration as unscientific, or less kindly as nonsense or quackery. Mimi, not one to follow the crowd, kept true to her philosophy. Her belief in the power of thought had served her well and her example had taught me so much.

In the summer of 1971, Mimi began complaining of pain in her upper back. Occasionally, I was asked to drive her to a doctor. She dismissed the problem in front of me, not wanting me to worry. At first, Mimi dealt with her acute aches as more of a nuisance than something serious, let alone life-threatening. Now and then a grimace would grip her face when the pain set in.

Pain can age the young and devastate the old. Although she

did her best to go on with her daily life as usual, the signs were not good. Her appetite waned. Her self-assured walk become hesitant and she moved more slowly. She tired easily and began taking rests in the middle of the day. This was not the vigorous, unstoppable Mimi I had grown up with. At first, I tried to rationalize it away: Mimi was just going through the normal aches and pains associated with getting older, nothing abnormal was going on. I wanted to believe this with all my heart.

If I ever had a hint that she was under the weather, it would blow over before I had a chance to think about it, let alone worry about her being ill. But when Mimi began seeing doctors, I had to face the truth. The torment was too serious for her mind/body philosophy to handle alone. To hear Mimi admit that she was confronting a power stronger than herself was devastating. Although I didn't want to face the fact that Mimi had a serious problem, it was clearly time to worry.

An air of foreboding hung over me as I drove my grandmother on her appointed rounds: One office visit after another, one doctor's face after another, one painful examination after another, one disappointment after another. Mimi suffered while the doctors remained unanimous in their collective worthless and frustrating diagnosis: "I can't find anything that could be causing this pain."

This was long before the disease detecting technology of CAT scans and MRIs that we routinely take for granted today. These diagnostic marvels would not be approved by the Federal Drug Administration until the early '80s—too late to help Mimi. She continued suffering, mostly in silence. Her family suffered along as well. We were distraught. What on earth was hurting our dear Mimi?

Doctors in the Dark: The Phantom Pain

During her two-year search for help and relief, doctors repeatedly told Mimi that nothing was wrong. Although her doctors had found nothing wrong, there was one physician who believed the pain was real even without knowing the cause. Mimi was thankful that, at least, he acknowledged her suffering. He prescribed pain medications, shots in the dark that did little to ease her distress.

Back in the '70s, doctors were more restricted in prescribing pain medicines than they are today, especially when the cause of the pain couldn't be isolated. Fear of patient addiction by the medical establishment so outweighed the cry for rational pain management that many people suffered for no good reason. Although not one to take medications, my grandmother took the painkillers, which the doctor had prescribed, hoping for relief that would never come—at least not from medication.

Mimi was now in constant agony. Her life had become a form of hell. I was sure she'd end up seeing every doctor in Texas. Her gentle, fragile spirit was screaming for help and the doctors couldn't hear her. Today, it sounds nearly absurd that the army of doctors Mimi had consulted couldn't, at the very least, diagnose the source of her pain.

Although several doctors had alluded to it, one specialist really put his foot in his mouth. I was with Mimi when the doctor called her into his office after "carefully" examining her. He callously concluded: "Mrs. Friedman, I can't find anything physically wrong with you and I see that none of the other doctors you've seen have been able to either. It's not uncommon as we get older to develop ills that are really in our head."

Mimi shot me a look, letting me know she thought this doctor was crazy.

What arrogance! Instead of prescribing pain medication, this doctor wanted to put her on tranquilizers to snuff out the phantom pain. Mimi would have no part of a doctor who couldn't see that her pain was as real as his fee for services would soon be. She didn't return to that particular healer. She knew her pain was in her back, not her head. I knew it, too.

Mimi persisted in her pilgrimage, and the misdiagnosis game continued. One physician, without bothering to look for the underlying cause of the back pain, recommended she wear a corset to support her back and, thus, ease her pain. As I took Mimi from "doctor-do-nothing" to "doctor-do-little," I became increasingly disheartened by how limited the medical establishment was in diagnosing her problem. I had thought the doctors would persist in finding the cause and offer some comfort, if not a cure.

Another doctor thought she might have a pinched nerve in her back. The operative word here is "thought"—he guessed; he didn't know. He recommended a procedure involving injections of lidocaine, a numbing agent, that would temporarily anesthetize the area of her back that was torturing her from the inside out. The injections had, in some cases, brought long-lasting relief for people with chronic back pain stemming from muscular-skeletal problems such as herniated discs or arthritis-related complications.

The doctor described the treatment to Mimi. He didn't hold back on the details.

"First, Mrs. Friedman, you must lie face down and absolutely still on a table," said the doctor. "Then, I have to insert a needle into your back to . . ."

"Is it a long needle?" Mimi interrupted.

"Well, long enough," the doctor continued, "to numb the specific nerve that carries pain messages to the brain. You must

lie perfectly still throughout the entire procedure. Any movement could cause paralysis, or worse."

Mimi sighed.

I couldn't believe it. More pain to stop pain—maybe. The
irony of it all wasn't funny. The "cure" sounded like a chapter in
a book on medieval torture. I felt this treatment was horrible,
not knowing Mimi would have to stomach worse "cures" yet to
come. Then, more shock.

Mimi sat in the chair, fully composed, and said to the doctor
with the big needle, "Let's do it."

She had the painful injection treatments with the long needle but they did no good and actually made the pain worse.

"Is there a real doctor in the house?" I screamed inside.

Living with chronic suffering slowed Mimi down, but being a
woman of great inner strength, the pain didn't stop her from living an active life. Even now, as I write about her, it's difficult to
comprehend how much courage this woman was able to muster.
She would wake each morning and dress to greet the new day.
Mimi was not one to mope around my aunt and uncle's home in
a robe. She went about doing chores, tidying up, preparing most
of the meals, and often baby-sat with my children. At the time,
1972, my daughter, Michelle, was 2½ and my son, Randy, was 6
months old. I was twenty-seven.

Mimi would also go food shopping with me. At the grocery
store, we'd each grab a shopping cart and deposit one child in
each seat. We'd fill the carts to overflowing with food and all
the ingredients for our special recipes. I think back now and
wonder. How was she able to push those heavy carts? How was
she able to stand on her feet helping me cook for the family?
Where did she find the strength to help me in the midst of her
traumatizing pain? But cooking had always been her pleasure
and passion. She seemed to thrive, even look better, during our
cooking marathons together. Whenever I reflect on those days
when my grandmother helped me cook, I still marvel at her

tenacity for holding onto life and giving her family joy at a cost I doubt many would be willing to pay.

Before Mimi became ill, my life was as happy as any life could be. I was fortunate that I was able to be an at-home mother. Being a mother was all I had ever wanted to be. Mimi and my mother were my role models. Life was perfect.

Mimi loved my children and the feeling was mutual. Michelle always greeted Mimi with outstretched hands, begging to be picked up and held in the comfort of her loving arms. She played with them, often sliding onto the floor where she'd sing, laugh and talk with them. She was a hands-on great-grandmother. Always a mother at heart, she changed diapers, gently and patiently fed Randy one spoonful at a time, and helped me put the kids to bed when Stan was working late.

Although she was hurting all the time, Mimi was always willing to baby-sit. She would light up when she was with Michelle and Randy, and I'm certain those cherished moments with them helped her cope with the relentless pain. I'll never forget the day Mimi took me aside and confessed, "Mary Ann, dear, I can't lift your babies." I was terrified. Now I really knew that Mimi was losing her fight.

Chapter 5

❧

Madame Curie,
I Presume

"Doctors think a lot of patients are cured who have simply quit in disgust." —Don Herold

In 1972, a doctor finally figured out that Mimi's pain was not in her head. It was in her back, as she'd been saying for two agonizing years. Since Mimi's pain had gotten much worse over time, the doctor decided to take an X ray of her chest. Why this simple diagnostic test hadn't been suggested earlier by one member of the seemingly endless procession of doctors is still a mystery to me.

The X ray exposed a suspicious mass on Mimi's lung. The doctor called for a biopsy, which would soon tell us whether the growth was harmless or malignant.

Although I didn't comprehend the complete significance of the operation that would remove a bit of her lung for the biopsy, I felt relieved. After two horrendous years, Mimi was, at last, getting the medical attention she so desperately needed. At the same time, I was angry with the medical establishment and the doctors I had trusted. How could they have let her suffer for so long without exploring every option until they found the cause? An X ray was all it took. For the first time in my life I began to comprehend firsthand that doctors have considerable limitations.

Here We Sit

On the day of the biopsy, my anger at the doctors had given way to fear. I was scared to death of what the surgeon might find. My entire family had assembled in the hospital waiting room. The walls were flat and empty; the chairs were hard and uninviting. My mother and my aunt Marie sat together as if combining their strength could somehow pull their mother through this ordeal. Uncle Jack and my cousins, Susie and Joan, were all there. My brother, Steve, his wife, Gail, and their twin daughters, were in Houston waiting for the call. My children were too young to be at the hospital and were in good hands with my dear friend Joni.

We waited—a collective of people called a family. If you think about it, waiting means remaining in one place for an outcome, stalled in a never-never land of some expectation. That was how we all felt. It was a troubled wait. We talked and laughed, anything to keep us from thinking about why we were here. But our mind games were merely a veneer—our attempts at distraction weren't working. We all knew it without having to say it. We couldn't fool ourselves. We were all worried about Mimi.

My 66-year-old father was sitting next to me. Deep concern was etched on his face; he could never hide his emotions. His hand rested on the armchair beside me and I cupped my hand over his and gently stroked it. Although Mimi was his mother-in-law, I believe he couldn't have loved her more if she had been his own mother. She was the delicate thread of gold and strength that held this family together.

The Moment of Truth

After what seemed like ages, I looked up and saw the doctor coming toward the waiting room. We jumped to our feet and were out in the hallway before the doctor had a chance to call out our name. The entire clan formed a circle around him in the hallway, but his cheerless face said everything before he had a chance to say one word.

"I'm sorry," said the surgeon, "She has lung cancer."

The words reverberated in my head, and a sick feeling overwhelmed me.

"It's small cell cancer," he continued, "which is a very virulent form. She has no more than three to six months to live. I'm sorry. This is the worst kind of cancer. It grows very fast and there is nothing we can do."

Tears flooded my eyes. I fell into my father's arms crying out, "No, not my Mimi! How can we get along without her?"

This couldn't be happening. I was having a nightmare. If only I could wake up. We all tried dealing with the horrible news while trying to console one another at the same time. That one sentence from her doctor consumed my entire family with grief.

My thoughts immediately turned to my children. Randy and Michelle were so young; they'd never remember my Mimi. They would never know the joy, the wisdom, and the sweet beauty that was her.

True Lies

After my family recovered from the initial shock of Mimi's impending end, Aunt Marie and Mother decided that my grandmother didn't need to know she had terminal cancer. Since she had no estate to "put in order," why burden Mimi with the painful inevitable? As the logic of the suggestion seemed to make sense, I embraced the comfort of denial. It was agreed. We wouldn't tell her she was dying. What would be gained? This was a tricky ethical issue. To tell, or not to tell, that was the question.

I don't know what story my grandmother was told. "Don't ask, don't tell" seemed to be the order of the day. Since she never asked me what was wrong with her, I never had to lie. But you know the saying, you can run but you can't hide. A heavy unspoken truth placed a raw edge on the precious little time we had together. Mimi and I could both feel the specter of death—it was palpable.

I had made a decision. I was determined to spend as much time with my grandmother as I could. Recovering from the biopsy took Mimi quite a while. She felt so bad after the surgery that I thought she was going to expire any moment. Since the doctors said she had only a few months to live, I assumed that she was, in fact, dying. But gradually, and to my amazement, she improved. Pretty soon she was nearly back to her old self. Although she still had chronic pain, she had regained her strength. Despite the enormous pain drain on her poor body, Mimi's recuperative powers were astonishing. She had a great will to live. It seemed that life had returned to perfect. We were able to shop and have fun once again. It almost felt as if the cancer had disappeared—almost.

Who Were We Kidding?

Now that the cause of the pain had been found, Mimi underwent radiation and chemotherapy—an ordeal in itself. Her doctors didn't expect these protocols to lengthen her life; they hoped the treatments would reduce the escalating pain and make her life more bearable during the brief time she had left. This was not good news. After wanting to know the truth for so long, I now had it and I was miserable.

Looking back, who did we think we were kidding? She must have known she had cancer—especially Mimi, a person whose mind and body were well connected. The body has an innate wisdom and knows when something is seriously wrong. You know it and I know it. She wasn't undergoing these cancer-killing treatments for a bad cold. Still, the word, "cancer," remained unspoken. Mimi seemed okay with it, too.

Our silence had another motive and I'm sure she had figured that out as well. Mimi knew our code of silence was meant not only to shield her from the truth, but to protect all of us who loved her so much from our own pain. If we didn't tell her she was going to die from cancer, we could remain in that duty-free zone of denial where the cancer would go away and she would live on happily ever after as in a fairy tale. Denial is one of those textbook first-stage reactions that people go through after learning a loved one has a terminal disease. Denial can be a wonderful drug, though it often comes at a high price.

Always Brave

Mimi became dreadfully sick from the chemotherapy. Thirty years ago, there were no effective drugs available to ease the nausea, vomiting, and weakness. The treatments were awful, leaving her sick and weak. She also lost her appetite and got progressively thinner. But as sick as she was from these treatments, she didn't take her fate lying down. Death stared at her and she stared right back without blinking.

To my wishful and wistful eyes, my ailing dear Mimi appeared to be strong. I was seeing through those proverbial rose-colored glasses. Later on, after Mimi had died, my aunt told me that there were many times when my grandmother would awaken in the middle of the night so sick to her stomach that they'd rush her to the hospital emergency room, where a shot of morphine would be given to settle her nausea and vomiting. Brave Mimi never burdened me with descriptions of those attacks or complained about her health. At the time, I never knew about her late night emergency room visits.

What could I do to help her? As I've said, cooking was a tradition between grandmother and granddaughter. Cooking nourished our bodies, fed our spirits, gave us strength, and deepened our love. With Randy on my hip and with Michelle off at preschool, I would whip up a selection of many different recipes for Mimi's lunch. Then I'd wrap them up and rush over to my aunt's house with the hope that one of those dishes would soothe and nourish Mimi's weakening body. My husband came home for lunch every day to watch Randy so I could make my special food run.

I'd sit in a chair next to her bed while we watched her favorite soap opera. Sometimes, I'd lean back and watch my grandmother, knowing these tender images of Mimi would have to last a lifetime.

Despite her illness, we could still make gold out of straw. We were alchemists when it came to cooking. We could create special memories from small things, even those meant to alleviate the ravages of her cancer treatments. Even 30 years later, the aroma of ginger snap cookies immediately sparks the memory of watching *Another World* while Mimi and I dunked ginger snap cookies in our coffee. Ginger, a traditional remedy for motion sickness, was also recommended to help counter the acute nausea that routinely followed chemotherapy.

We were living, seeing, sensing, and appreciating the value

of life. As it was happening and unfolding before me, I was a witness to how Mimi and I were taking delight in the details of our shared moments, scenes of my grandmother forever framed and embedded like photographs in my consciousness. I knew we had entered a different way of perceiving time as it was happening. We made the most of everything. Helping Mimi was giving me an education you can't find in the best universities.

Chapter 6

Denial Works! A Fool's Paradise

"We understand death for the first time when he puts his hand upon one whom we love." —Madame De Stael

Although it may not be the best approach for issues we'd rather sweep under the rug, denial with a conscious motive does work to numb your reality. As long as you know you're fooling yourself, you won't be totally devastated and you won't suffer mortal shock when you and fate finally collide.

Denial had worked to ease the pain of Mimi's family at the inevitable outcome of her illness. Perhaps it would have been better to tell her the truth so she could have been prepared. Maybe we had underestimated her ability to handle the facts. Maybe we could have done more to fight the disease if we would have broken our "code of silence." In our denial as a family, we were living in a temporary fool's paradise and Mimi was paying the high-priced rent.

Six months passed quickly. Mimi didn't die as predicted. The cancer was still there and so was she—looking thin and haggard—but still alive and kicking. My grandmother didn't know that she was supposed to die in six months. The seed to self-destruct at an appointed time had not been planted in her mind, so she didn't cooperate in fulfilling the prophecy of her doctors.

Mimi had not died as predicted by the experts. She was un-aware of the date connected with her impending doom and in-nocent enough for her belief system to work on automatic pilot. I, and as I would later learn my mother as well, was learning an important lesson from Mimi that would color my perspective about life and influence my decisions for years to come—espe-cially my refusal to accept arbitrary limits placed in our paths by others.

However, despite the chemotherapy and radiation, Mimi's pain continued to increase. Oral medications were fast waning in potency and no longer kept her pain at a tolerable level. I don't know how she endured the agony. Her dark sunken eyes spoke volumes; she wasn't sleeping much. Waking up to excru-ciating pain in the middle of the night is a living nightmare that no healthy person could ever truly imagine. If it were me, I think I'd be crying out from the pain. Not Mimi. She was one tough lady. She kept going and managed to maintain a sem-blance of a productive life.

Although I never saw her so much as flinch in public, I had a theory that she had devised her own way of coping. When she would find herself all alone in my aunt's house, I imagined that she would feel liberated enough to cry out. Being alone in her daughter's home, her wails wouldn't impose her anguish on any-one. Yes, I thought, it would be just like my sweet grandmother to hold in all the pain until she could scream out and release the suffering in private.

Later, I learned from my mother that Mimi did succumb to the pain. When her suffering became intolerable, she'd cry out in desperation. Aunt Marie or Uncle Jack would rush her to the St. Joseph's Hospital where the nurses, who were nuns, would medicate her with morphine.

Finally, Mimi required regular morphine injections for pain. The pills, which had done little to moderate the pain in the first place, now did absolutely nothing for her. Rather than taxing poor Mimi's body by frequently dragging her off to the hospital for her injections, her doctor prescribed that she receive them at home. But this solution presented another problem: someone at home needed to give her the injections. Even though I wanted to be the one to help with her pain, I couldn't bring myself to actually push a needle into my grandmother's body. At the time, I was too squeamish. I suppose if I had been the last resort, I'd have given her those shots. When one of my gutsy cousins, Joan, who lived nearby, volunteered for injection duty, I was grateful and relieved for Mimi, and for my wimpy self.

When push does come to shove we are all capable of unpredictable and marvelous accomplishments. For the impatient among us, keep in mind that things evolve at their own pace and progress may take years to unfold. But if we are open to the challenge of change and growth, life will surprise us. If I could have gazed into the future with the help of a crystal ball, I would have been astonished to see what I had become. Seventeen years later, I would find my true calling to become a doctor who routinely gave injections. Unlike Mimi's crippling pain that she couldn't will into oblivion, being squeamish about injections was just a thought in my head that I had the power to change. It just took a long time to find the motivation that comes from within.

Despite the chemotherapy, radiation, nausea, and unspeakable pain, Mimi never talked about her illness and the word "cancer" never came up—the loving conspiracy of silence was gently and delicately maintained by all. I don't know what Mimi was thinking about her declining health. There were many times when I wanted to talk to her about the cancer, the end of life, and what she thought about the hereafter, but I didn't. Maybe I didn't give my grandmother enough credit for knowing more than I knew. Maybe silence was the coward's way out. For certain, I missed out on her insights into the realities we all must one day confront.

Even though I was grateful for every precious minute I had with Mimi, it was heartbreaking to watch this vibrant woman withering before my eyes. I knew the end was creeping up in the shadows. Mimi was getting thinner and was staying in bed more and more. Death was pushing its way into my world and neither Mimi nor I could push it back. But knowing the inevitable and accepting it are not the same. Knowing death was at Mimi's door, I still couldn't imagine life without her. If she died, I knew a part of me would die too.

The upcoming days, weeks, and months of uncertainty were going to test us all.

Chapter 7

Treasures Not Buried

"It seems simple to me, but for some people I guess feeling takes courage." —Aretha Franklin

When I married Stan in 1969, Mimi had given me her treasured wedding ring, the one young Will Friedman had slipped onto her finger 57 years earlier. She told me to use the band during my wedding, but not to wear it as my wedding band afterward. Because Will had died so young, she felt her marriage was unlucky and didn't want the same for me. Although I didn't believe in such things, I followed my grandmother's instructions and only wore the ring that one day. After all, even smart folks can be superstitious.

It was now four years later and Mimi was about to die. I thought she would want to wear her wedding band as she followed her husband Will into the next incarnation. Mimi was lying in her bed, so weak and frail, and I was tongue-tied. How do I ask her if she wants to be buried with her wedding band if we haven't even acknowledged that she was dying? Finally, I simply said, "Mimi, I still have your wedding band. Do you want it back?"

When she heard that I wanted to return the ring, she surprised me. "No. Listen, Mary Ann, I want you to have it," she said, putting the band back in my hand. At that very moment, I knew beyond any doubt that Mimi knew the truth. She knew she was dying. She was entrusting that part of her past into a future that she would not be part of—at least not in the physical sense. With the formality of passing the wedding band to me, she was saying, "Take this part of me with you." With a simple "Thank you," I placed the gold band on my finger and never again took it off. My grandmother's band of gold was a legacy, an heirloom I would always cherish. It represents my connection to Mimi. With her band on my finger, I feel that Mimi is always with me.

The Pain Continues

When the malignant pain became unbearable for Mimi to endure at home, she would stay in the hospital where they could monitor her vital signs as they gave her increased doses of morphine.

"She might become addicted," said one nurse, parroting what the doctors of those days thought about these drugs.

I found this attitude absurd and downright stupid. Although my grandmother had a terminal illness and had already outlived all expectations, the medical personnel at the hospital were afraid to give her too much pain medication.

So what if she did become addicted? She was going to die! What was the problem here? She wouldn't be addicted for long.

Whenever I was around, Mimi tried being stoical but, in front of my mother, Cele, she would let her distress show. Cele spent most of the time with her mother when she was hospitalized. My mother told me that, at times, Mimi's pain became so excruciating that her screams would pierce the silence of the hospital corridor—sending my mother running for a nurse. The dosage of morphine the nurses gave Mimi allowed her to teeter

at a notch just below torture. I call this cruel and unusual pun-
ishment for the innocent. She was never given enough medication to put the pain at bay, to allow her to catch her breath, to
allow her body to rest from the torment.

Despite all our pleading for help, Mimi was denied the medication that would ease her horrible misery. Cele constantly asked
the nurses to give Mimi more pain medication. They didn't.

After Mimi had returned home from one of her agonizing
bouts at the hospital, she didn't just sit in her room full of self-
pity. Instead, she looked up a salesman who once worked in my
uncle's furniture store. My aunt had remembered that this salesman dabbled in hypnosis. After a few sessions with him, Mimi
said the hypnosis did help relax her. She was on the right track.
She knew if she could find someone to help focus her mental
powers, she'd have a considerable edge in fighting her illness. In
the hands of a professional hypnotherapist, Mimi would surely
have fared even better.

Mary Ann's Soapbox

Ironically, Mimi, born in the 19th century, was truly a modern woman trapped in the latter half of the 20th century—
which was backward in so many ways, especially when it came
to pain control. Hypnotism in the early '70s in the Southwest
was not exactly widely accepted as a medical tool. Hypnosis suffered from negative press and misconceptions associated with
charlatans, spooky trancelike states, séances, and entertainment
popularized on television and in the movies.

Mimi knew better. Hypnosis was no oddball supernatural
notion or a shadowy demon hiding in the realm of the psyche.
She intuitively knew hypnosis was a catalyst for unleashing the
power of suggestion. There's no doubt that the power of sugges-

tion is real. How many of us have experienced feeling itchy while watching a film about bugs, or when we thought our beloved dog had been infested by fleas? How many of us have read our daily horoscope and had a great day when it said we'd have one? Or, conversely, how many of us have read a horoscope that hinted at a bad day and we sabotaged ourselves into fulfilling the prediction? The power of suggestion is one of the most misunderstood tools of the mind to this day. Remember the adage: It's mind over matter.

Although time was not on Mimi's side, time would prove her right. Today, the link between hypnosis, guided imagery and the power of suggestion and its effects on the body and mind is science. Hypnotherapists, no longer considered disreputable hucksters, help people quit smoking, lose weight, reduce stress, build confidence, improve the immune system, and achieve many other worthwhile goals. The furniture salesman and hypnosis dabbler who worked for my uncle and tried helping Mimi had also been on the right track. Pioneers in all fields have been called crazy, quacks, or worse by those warming the benches on the sidelines since time immemorial.

Modern Western medicine has had a checkered history when it comes to assessing what is best for the patient. Allowing the frail and sick to suffer is heinous. Why couldn't the poor souls in their last days receive the pain medication that would give them peace and comfort? The horrible and needless pain my poor grandmother had endured was shaping my view of the medical arts as it coexists with the politics and big business of healing.

Taking in the larger picture, I can see it wasn't totally the fault of Mimi's doctor that she didn't receive the pain medication she so desperately needed. Fearing their state medical licensing board will revoke their license for patient drug abuse, physicians are generally hesitant to prescribe certain levels of pain medication. Whatever happened to the doctor and patient privilege? Who determines an arbitrary value on what type of painkiller is prescribed, or what dosage is too much? You can be sure it's not the person in pain who is splitting such hairs, or worrying about addiction. If revoking a doctor's license for prescribing the very drug and dosage a patient needs sounds crazy, it is. Little in this country has substantially changed when it comes to the business of health and the bureaucracy of pain management since Mimi's days. Recently, a doctor confided that he still feels that same concern about giving his patients the pain medication they actually need.

Of course, there are drug abuse cases out there and some doctors prescribe highly addictive pain medications indiscriminately. Should society make incontestable decisions for everyone based on the abuses of a few? I think you know by now what Mimi would say. Beware legislators who want to protect you from yourself. When discretion is replaced with reducing everything to its lowest common denominator, we get the tyranny of the masses, a fascist mentality deciding what's best for all of us, doctors who give patients so many months to live and health maintenance organizations driven by the bottom line. What grand purpose was there for my sweet Mimi to suffer needlessly because others had abused drugs? Such dull and dense thinking by the medical community-at-large has historically been ill-advised and is deplorable in an enlightened and free society.

Witnessing firsthand all the nonsense regarding Mimi's interminable search for a proper diagnosis and pain management by committee was an education in the trenches of health care. The seeds of my future values and career were being sowed without me being aware of it.

Chapter 8

❧

The Cost of Living

"Courage is often the outcome of despair as of hope; in the one case we have nothing to lose, in the other everything to gain."
—Diane de Poitiers

Despite torturous pain and no relief in the foreseeable future, Mimi wanted to live. Even in pain she didn't wish herself to die. Even though she surely knew by now that she was dying, she never gave in to that thought. She just wanted to live as long as she could. She was a fighter.

Mimi's doctor was amazed. He told us he could not believe she was still alive. Two years had passed since her terminal cancer diagnosis and prognosis of no more than six short months to live. Given her predicament—alive and in awful pain—he suggested that she undergo a medical procedure that would block the nerve area carrying pain signals to the brain.

The joyous idea of finally stopping Mimi's excruciating pain sounded like a wish come true until I heard the grisly details. The operation was difficult, painful, and dangerous—three strikes that would make anyone think twice. The doctor told Mimi there was a chance that she might not live through the operation. He had to go through her neck and sever the nerve in her back at the specific vertebra that would block the transmission of her pain. Despite the pain inflicted by the procedure, it was imperative that she not move a muscle at the risk of becoming paralyzed. To make matters worse, they couldn't sedate Mimi for the procedure. Because she was already taking morphine on a regular basis for the pain, giving her an additional sedative might kill her.

After listening to the gory details, Mimi, without hesitation, decided to go for it. She told my mother that if there was any chance of relieving the pain, she wanted to try it. If this palliative procedure might alleviate the pain, she would gamble against death and take the odds under the surgeon's knife. Anyone agreeing to this risky and excruciating operation had to be in unspeakable agony.

The procedure was scheduled right after Mother's Day, 1975. While we didn't discuss her illness or her dying, we also didn't talk much about our feelings. Although Mimi and I didn't speak of it, our relationship was so close that it never seemed necessary to say "I love you" out loud. Now that she was dying I was afraid to say it, afraid to tip her off that something was wrong, that she wasn't long for this world—a situation than can scare the bravest soul. I knew that she knew how I felt. Words were not necessary.

While we weren't a touchy-feely kind of family, we were always there for each other. Still, I had things to say, things I wanted Mimi to embrace. I decided I'd convey my feelings for her in a Mother's Day poem. I wrote down all the things that had been important to me, all the things I could remember that she had done for me. My poem started with: "A Grandmother is someone who tells you to put on a sweater when she is cold. A Grandmother tells you to eat your vegetables because children in other parts of the world were starving. A Grandmother babysits for her great-grandchildren." I went on to list about twenty different things that she did for me. I was acknowledging her contribution to my life. I was letting her know that she wasn't taken for granted. I was scared she wouldn't survive the procedure and wanted to express my deep appreciation of her before the operation—just in case. I slipped my ode to Mimi under her pillow in the hospital room while she was sleeping. Later, she thanked me for the card and told me how much she liked it.

The procedure was a success and her pain subsided dramatically. I was thankful that I had worried for nothing. Because she could now begin functioning with less morphine in her system, she was more alert. The Mimi I knew had returned to me. I was thrilled. Maybe the doctors had been wrong all along. With her pain blocked, her eyes looked rested for the first time in years. It seemed to me that she had canceled her appointment with death.

Addictions and the Hereafter

I've come to learn that when you solve one problem, other problems can occur as a consequence. Although the pain had now been blocked, Mimi still had cancer. Now, she had also become addicted to morphine, which was par for the course in such situations. With the operation a success, Mimi had to be weaned from the morphine circulating in her system, and it had to be done gradually.

She would remain in the hospital until her body's craving for morphine had subsided. After what seemed like an eternity to me—I can't conceive of what it seemed to Mimi—a light at the end of a long, dark tunnel shone brightly and steadily. Mimi still had cancer, but somehow I felt that would go away, too.

But I had become addicted to denial. I preferred it and there were no federal laws against it. Many people live for years with cancer still in their body; some go into remission for years; and others manifest miraculous spontaneous cures—I wanted to believe she would be a member of the latter group. Although I had never given up hope that Mimi would live, I'd have bouts of uncontrollable crying and depression, a dark feeling I tried hiding from my family. I was on an emotional roller coaster.

My mother knew me very well. She could see me shifting emotionally. I was drifting from unbridled hope to despair. She saw that I wasn't managing my grief any better now than I had after the shock of the initial diagnosis two years back. One day, while Mother and I were in the car driving somewhere, I started sobbing that I just couldn't live without Mimi. Mother pulled the car over and put the car in park. "You're going to have to learn to deal with this, Mary Ann. Maybe you should get some professional help." Get help? The words hit me hard. I felt as if I'd smashed into an emotional brick wall.

I took my mother's advice and spoke with my religious leader, an older gentleman whom I respected. He and Mimi had become friends during his many visits with her in the hospital. He admired Mimi a great deal. He watched her fight to live, enduring so much pain in order to keep living. I was sure he would understand my fear of losing her. I was sure he'd heard the same lament from all those who had loved ones facing death.

He told me that Mimi derived the strength and will necessary to fight the cancer from the love of her family, and he encouraged me to keep on expressing my love for her. His words were reassuring, yet he couldn't tell me what I wanted to hear most—that Mimi would not die.

Mimi gained strength from our love. I keyed in on that powerful mind/body concept. I decided my grandmother needed me to help her find the answers that she would look for if she could.

I began reading everything about death—from clairvoyant Edgar Cayce to Elizabeth Kubler-Ross who introduced the "stages of dying" or "stages of grief" model which is still widely quoted. Reading about death and dying would help me more than it would help Mimi. I did have a knack for research and forged ahead.

In the early '70s, the phenomenon of near-death experiences

documented by Kubler-Ross and others, which had been reported for thousands of years in cultures around the globe, suddenly captured the public's interest and began making news in the mass media. I was drawn to these reports out of the need to believe there would be a time in the future when I'd see Mimi again; just the thought of such a heavenly reunion felt like a soothing salve on my aching heart. Articles, books, lectures and workshops about near-death and out-of-body experiences seemed to be sprouting up across the country for a growing spiritual market. Perhaps those articles had always been there. Since I hadn't been looking for them, I hadn't noticed they existed. There is little doubt that we see what we want to see. Although there are variations of near-death experiences and no two are identical, a general pattern is undeniable. We now know a person whose heart has stopped and appears dead isn't really dead—at least not in that moment. There is a five- or six-minute window of opportunity to save that life.

During that time, many people feel themselves rising out of their own bodies while observing their surroundings, including their mortal bodies below—often in an ambulance or a hospital emergency room. These fortunate people described how they watched dispassionately as EMTs, doctors and nurses tried saving them with CPR or with an external defibrillator—a device that delivers short electrical currents to shock the heart back into a normal rhythm. We've all seen these scenes depicted on TV and in the movies—a doctor yells "clear," the pads of the defibrillator are applied to the patient's chest, the shock is given, and the monitor beeps if the heart is beating again and the patient has come back to life. A persistent flat line on the monitor requires no dialogue.

Many who have experienced near-death experiences report seeing a bright light at the end of a long tunnel and being greeted by family and friends who had died before them. Naturally, the meaning and significance of this phenomenon

was, and still is, analyzed to "death." The World Wide Web has
many sites devoted to forums about near-death encounters.

It's possible the near-death experience is strictly physical, a
biochemical-generated hallucination created by the brain to
confront the end of corporeal existence. As I read through all
the near-death material I could get my hands on, there was no
way to absolutely and empirically prove the implication—that
there is life after death. I had made my decision. These near-
death stories were more than the fantasies of dying people, or
faith in the hereafter. Too many people from around the world
and from varied cultures and religions had reported similar
near-death scenarios to dismiss the experience as mass hypnosis,
or even coincidence—which would be a stretch.

Something real happened to all those souls who had faced
the other side of life, something that was helping me cope with
Mimi's future, with my future. The near-death tales of others
gave me a great psychological lift and hope. At least, I said to
myself, if Mimi was going to die I could count on seeing her
again. I was following Mimi's lead. We do create our own realities and that's not an opinion—it's a fact of life we prove to ourselves every day.

Chapter 9

❧

Letting Go

"How lucky I am to have known somebody that saying good-bye to is so damn bad." —Jill Kimentz, *The Other Side of the Mountain*

I believe my determination to keep Mimi alive did help keep her alive. I believe she lived on in great part because I needed her. I wouldn't let death slip in like a thief in the night and steal her away—not on my watch. But with all the good my positive attitude brought to Mimi and me, I began feeling that my questionable hold on my grandmother wasn't fair to her. Poor Mimi had been in such pain for so long that she might have let go of this life a lot sooner had it not been for my unspoken insistence that she live—no matter the cost to her.

After reading all about the near-death experiences and feeling that this life on earth was not our only existence, I finally realized that I had to come to grips with her death and I chucked denial out the window. I could let her go in peace.

In the midst of my distress about facing Mimi's death, something in me settled down, like the calm after a violent storm. I came to a conclusion. The truth was that I wouldn't know how I would deal with her death until she died—anything else was intellectual speculation. You can't think how you will feel. Acknowledging this point was the beginning of my letting go. If Mimi needed to leave her world of pain behind, then I had to respect her silent entreaty for redemption. After spending two years mourning my still-alive grandmother, I saw that there are worse things than death. Asking her to live in hell was not how I wanted to love her. I needed to let Mimi go. In my mind and with a very sad heart, I did.

Two days after I made that quiet, private decision, my dear, sweet, loving grandmother, was in pain no more.

On the morning of May 21, 1975, the nun on duty came to give Mimi, who was still being weaned off the morphine, her shot of methadone. Mimi was sleeping peacefully as the nurse prepared the injection. But the nurse made a fatal mistake. If she had tried waking Mimi, she would have realized that a sizable dose of methadone was still in her system. With no malice intended, the nurse gave Mimi her methadone injection, accidentally inducing an overdose.

I remember getting a call from my mother. She told me that the hospital had called with a simple message that nearly stopped my heart. "Come to the hospital immediately."

By the time my mother, aunt, cousins and I arrived at the hospital, Mimi was gone. My grandmother never woke up after the methadone shot and died a death of the innocent. My fear had become real. I summoned my courage and I went into her room by myself. She was lying there as if only serenely asleep. It was now time for me to say good-bye. I bent down, kissed her on her still warm cheek, and said, "I love you, Mimi."

Although the pathology report stated that cancer was the cause of death, she had been killed by the methadone overdose. That bit of news was kept between us and the nurse who admitted it to us. It was a tragic mistake and she was devastated. What can you say? It went no further than that. We didn't sue the nurse, the doctors, their next of kin, their unborn children, the pharmaceutical company that produces methadone, or the hospital. I know this sounds out of sync and naïve in a society enchanted with civil litigation, including unfounded and costly malpractice suits. But we as a family felt our war had ended. We needed no more battles to deplete our life force. We all knew Mimi's time was very short. We also knew that her suffering had finally come to a merciful end. We let the overdose go and that was the wise choice for all concerned.

I don't remember much of the funeral service. I was there, yet the details of who said what or what happened next are murky—I can almost see them, but not quite. Several of Mimi's nurses from the hospital where she died and where she had spent so much time had come to pay their respects. They told us it was highly unusual for them to attend a patient's funeral. Mimi's nurses had such respect for her that they chose to make an exception and honor her memory in person.

I looked at Mimi's body in the open coffin and immediately recoiled, wishing I hadn't looked. I didn't want my last vision of her to be this body that had been dressed and made up by a mortician who didn't know her. Sobbing, I moved away from the coffin, away from this stiff, lifeless, body that was not my Mimi.

At the cemetery, I stood among grieving family members and friends as the eulogy spoke of her two-year fight with cancer and the words that brought it all home for me: "She fought so hard, not because she feared death but because she so loved life." This was true, I thought, as my grandmother was lowered into the earth. I also knew she had fought to live because I wouldn't let her go. My psychic grip on my grandmother was powerful. Thought is powerful. How right my Mimi was. Mimi continued to breathe in life through all the suffering until, in my selfish heart, I could let her go. As she was laid to rest, I felt no peace. A part of me was being buried, too.

The night after her funeral I couldn't sleep. I sat in the living room lit only by a dim lamp thinking about Mimi. Then, I got inspired. I picked up a pen and began writing down my thoughts and feelings about her—as if I could ever forget her. Yet, getting down the details was important. We can forget the details with the years. The mantra of "never again" became my newfound conviction. I vowed *never again* to put my needs ahead of someone else's pain. I would *never again* consciously send that manipulating message to someone I love. I would never again tell someone I love that they cannot die just because I couldn't deal with the loss. Something inside me was waking up.

Chapter 10

But This Is My Mother

"[t]he daughter never gives up on the mother, just as the mother never gives up on the daughter." —Rachel Billington

Eighteen years later, much had changed and much had remained the same. In fact, to my horror, my nightmare was happening all over again.

I felt as if I were on stage in some existential play with no way out. While Daddy and I were cast in the same roles, this time the part of the ailing loved one was not Mimi but Mimi's daughter who was having the biopsy. It was my 75-year-old mother, Cele, who, we were told, could have lung cancer.

Daddy and I were now in the same post-surgical waiting room of All Saints Hospital where Mimi had had the biopsy revealing she had lung cancer. Back then, the sparse walls and hard chairs in the waiting room had only intensified my fears. Now, nearly two decades later, the soft, warm pink color on the walls decorated with floral paintings and the padded chairs that cradled my body did nothing to alleviate my apprehension or anxiety. I was just as scared now as when my grandmother had been a patient here.

Dog-eared magazines were piled here and there on tables as they had been eighteen years earlier; other people in the room wore those same tight faces of concern with different style clothes;

everything, I felt, seemed to be nearly the same. Maybe it was me who was the same. If only I could wake from this dream, if only I could make life the way I wanted it to be. I was stuck in the meaningless groove called: If only.

Daddy and I sat under harsh soulless overhead lights that cast no shadows in the post-operative waiting room, a chamber full of palpable hope and unbearable uncertainty. The antiseptic smells were more than unpleasant; they reminded me this was as much a place of death as it was of recovery. But I knew that cure was inexorably connected to hope. And hope is one of the finer graces that makes us human and keeps us sane.

Then, there were the sounds. Doctors and nurses, who seemed much younger now than when Mimi had been incarcerated here, being paged relentlessly over the scratchy sound system was a constant reminder of why we were here. Although Daddy, the quiet romantic, had drifted off into his own world, I knew he was keenly aware of every smell and sound that assaulted us.

Let it be a false alarm, I prayed with all my heart. After Mimi died, I had vowed to put my own anguish aside. There is a time to let go. There is a time to die. I would never tell someone I love that they couldn't leave me.

Well, there's a reason for the saying, "never say 'never'." The vulture of absolutism was circling, waiting for me to slip up.

My mother was under the knife. The chill kept my backbone stiff. From my earliest memories, my mother had held me up when I was down. She held my hand and walked with me when I was afraid. My mother not only gave me life, she showed me how to live it with grace and appreciation.

Daddy and I waited in mutual silence. We were alone and together at the same time, which happens when people truly share an empathetic moment. Daddy and I were involved in something beyond time. In the post-operative waiting room, time was like a watched pot on the eternal brink of coming to a boil.

We waited for the diagnosis, the revelation. We waited to see the doctor coming toward us with a face that would say that the biopsy was negative and all was well. I could tell that Daddy was suffering both for Cele and himself. When he finally turned to speak to me, his usual bright eyes were glazed over and nearly lifeless, the words sticking in a dry mouth. "She has to be O.K."

What was I supposed to do? Should I reassure my 84-year-old father that he could go on without my mother? Often, the hardest thing is to simply listen and allow another person his feelings. Listening without judgment often paves the way for healing. I held Daddy's hand in mine. In the wink of the cosmic eye, I had become the parent and he the child.

Daddy sighed. His head tipped downward, locking into a frozen position as if he had gone into a waking trance. Let him do what he needs to do, I thought.

We waited together in that suffocating quiet space. I forced myself to be positive, to think good thoughts, to visualize my mother in perfect health. Yes, that was it. Mind over matter. Positive thinking might yet save the day as Mimi taught me. Whatever had brought my mother to this hospital, this place of disease, was nothing serious. These upbeat thoughts, however, sunk like dead weight in the face of what I was truly feeling in my secret harbor. I couldn't squelch that ominous and all too familiar gnawing in the pit of my stomach—that intuitive palpable experience that tells you something is not right.

Just one month earlier, Mother and Daddy had come home from a wonderful trip to Florida. Mother returned with good memories—and a nagging cough. Since she hadn't had a cold or any other related symptoms, Mother thought it was odd to have a respiratory problem. Like Mimi, Mother rarely complained or went to the doctor. She had a special intuition where her own health was concerned. She seemed to know when something was really wrong, when a symptom needed to be checked by a doctor. Like mother, like daughter.

After my mother had been examined by her doctor, he ordered an X ray that very day. Today, doctors don't wait around to see if a suspicious cough or other symptom will go away as they did when Mimi complained about the awful pain in her back. The American Cancer Society's public education program lists "a cough without a respiratory infection or other common reason" as a red flag and recommends having it thoroughly checked. It's always easier and smarter to nip things in the bud, as the saying goes. Mother's X ray revealed a large mass in the middle of her chest. Her doctor ordered an immediate biopsy of her lung.

Fast Forward

These were the events that had once again placed Daddy and me in the post-operative waiting room of that same hospital where Mimi had been 18 years ago, a heartbeat really when you truly love and remember.

I looked around the room. This time there were no uncles, aunts, and cousins to help lift our spirits by distracting us. Mother gave out the vibe that there was nothing to get worried about, so my brother, who lived in Houston, waited for the news at home.

I glanced over at my father. The skin on his face looked thin, fragile. My vigorous father now looked like an old man. Up until that moment, he had never looked old to me.

A biopsy in 1990 took far less time than the one Mimi and her family endured in 1972. You wait, knowing no news is still good news. Then, the moment arrives. The doctor's face tells the whole story. He had the same solemn expression that his counterpart, Mimi's doctor, had worn nearly two decades earlier.

The second blow falls like an ax. The words come and chop your world to pieces. "I'm sorry, she has lung cancer."

Daddy fell into my arms crying. "I can't live without her," he sobbed. I held him tightly, feeling stunned and shaken as tears of my own streamed down my face. If knowing is better than not knowing, then the worst was over. Daddy and I now knew were we stood. Mother would know soon enough.

I held onto Daddy, saying: "Look, this isn't her first bout with cancer. She beat the odds once, and she'll do it again."

I doubt that my father believed me.

Chapter 11

❦

Reality Is What You Decide It Is

"If I listened long enough to you, I'd find a way to believe that it's all true." —Rod Stewart

It was January in Texas—neither cold nor hot.

Unlike years ago, a lung biopsy was now an outpatient procedure—Mother had same-day service. As I drove Mother and Daddy home, the weight of the news seemed to put a drag on my accelerator. The familiar route appeared somehow skewed and different from what it had been only hours earlier when we were headed for the hospital. Now, my car crept along colorless streets that led us back to my parents' home. The sun that greeted us that morning had been replaced with a darkened sky dimmed by clouds both real and emotional. Mother, still a little sedated, was sufficiently alert and aware of her serious situation.

"It's not the same cell type that Mimi had," I said, reassuring Mother. "It's not as virulent."

"I see," Mother said. "What do they recommend?"

"We need to see a cancer specialist, an oncologist. There are options and treatments," I said in my most confident tone.

My car pulled us into the driveway. I felt numb. I had to leave. Duty called and I had to put on another hat. I had patients waiting to see me in my office. I kissed my mother goodbye. As I looked in the rearview mirror, tears filled my eyes. I drove off and considered staying home in case Mother needed me. But that would have frightened her even more. I needed to keep our daily routine as normal as possible. Mother would pick up on the slightest anomaly. I couldn't let on that I was seriously scared.

The doctor had told Daddy and me in private that my mother had only two months to live. I had heard that dirge before. The trumpets of death wail softly, hauntingly, and seductively like the Sirens of classical mythology who, with their fatal song, lured unfortunate sailors to their shipwrecked doom. Life is a choice of sink or swim, and I was treading water, hoping to remain afloat in a turbulent sea until we could reach a safe harbor. I knew if I drowned, so would my mother.

My world had been snatched out from under me once again. As far back as I can recall, my mother had never given me the sense that I was responsible for her. She had her life and I had mine to live. No guilt trips on her kids from Cele. It was precisely this attitude of love and emotional space that endeared her so much to me. She placed no burdens on me and neither did Daddy. I was a lucky child and a fortunate adult. If only I could throw a monkey wrench into the clock that was ticking off the moments of her life.

As I drove onto Granbury Road in southwest Fort Worth, everything seemed surrealistic. I tried to clear my aching head of the unstoppable river of thoughts and feelings. I tried thinking of anything except my dear mother's fate. I thought of my kids, my practice, my dog, love, cooking, the meaning of life, how strong we are, how fragile we are, my future. But it was no use. The specter of death kept returning. Thoughts inside my head were piling up in a bottleneck. I hit every red light. I felt stymied. I wanted to move. I wanted to find answers. I wanted action. But there I sat, waiting for a green light. Time was not on my side. I needed to collect my thoughts. I had to decide what action to take. I had to let my thoughts flow through me without judgment, without fighting them. Resistance in such matters is not only futile, it gives strength to the negative. Get out of your own way, Mary Ann, I thought to myself. The red light turned green and I moved on.

I surrendered to the reality that my mother was seriously ill. I could think of nothing else. I said to myself, trying to look for a positive crumb, trying to make sense out of chaos, at least she didn't have the more virulent small cell carcinoma that killed her mother. Cele had nonsmall cell adenocarcinoma, the most common lung cancer in women. Cele had been a social smoker who, although she never inhaled, had spent at least 25 years passively breathing in the secondhand smoke of others. My daddy, a long-term smoker, quit smoking when the Surgeon General's warning came out in 1964. Nonsmall cell was also the same cell type as the uterine cancer my mother had had 10 years earlier.

Cele, and thousands of other women, had been sucked up into the estrogen replacement treatment (ERT) hysteria of the '60s. During that period, the hormone, estrogen, was being touted by the pharmaceutical companies as the fountain of youth for those menopausal women who felt they were growing old. But it became alarmingly clear in the 1970s and '80s that this treatment was contributing to a tenfold increase in cancer of the uterus. My mother, Cele, became one of those grim statistics. After enduring radiation and surgery, she seemed to have beaten uterine cancer. My mother had been cancer free for a decade.

When we had a consultation meeting with the doctor who had diagnosed Cele's lung cancer, he informed us that surgery wasn't an option in Mother's case—the cancer had spread too far. He also speculated that a single cell from the uterine cancer may have somehow survived the treatment, remained dormant for 10 years, and had now spread to her lungs.

Another nightmare. The estrogen that triggered my mother's

uterine cancer may have now spawned and resurfaced as inoperable lung cancer. Unfortunately, the cancerous tumor had already spread or metastasized to the mediastinum—the area in
the middle of the chest outside the lungs. Cele's doctor concluded that the mediastal mass would kill her, not the cancer itself. The mass was lying dangerously close to the aorta blood
vessel, the pharynx and esophagus. Surgery was too risky. There
was a good chance of cutting the aorta and that meant instant
death.

If we did nothing, Cele's doctor felt that the growing oppres-
sive tumor would eventually press into the aorta, causing it to
burst, or push against the pharynx and suffocate her. Both scenarios offered a dreadful end. I certainly didn't want Mother to
suffer. I was afraid for her. The doctor offered Cele his reality.
Surgery was out and there was little else that could be done, except palliative radiation, which might extend her life six months.

There we go again with that "six months to live" prediction,
I thought. Maybe doctors should learn not to put limits on people's lives. I knew he was basing his prognosis on previous experiences and statistical data. But our bodies are not predictable
machines. You must treat the person, not only the disease. Each
one of us has a body that, under the right conditions, has the ca-
pacity to heal itself. I had learned that lesson. Doctors have no
crystal ball and no right to predict "time's up."

I wouldn't accept the prognosis.

Mimi had made liars of the doctors who thought she'd be
gone in a few months. She lived two full years beyond her doctor's best guess. Mimi had taught me that just as it is with food,
you have to develop a taste for life. Either you become a meat
and potatoes person, or a connoisseur. It's all up to you. Yes, you
can win if you've got the right stuff. I hoped my mother would
still feel that will to win, too. What people think of as impossible only means that it hasn't been done yet. I was a doctor now

myself. I knew doctors don't know everything. No one can predict how long someone will live. This time I knew better. Cele's lung cancer would be handled differently. When you're driving along alone in the car, all things seem possible as you create reality inside a landscape of dreams.

While pulling into the parking lot at the contemporary two-story professional office building where my clinic is located, I was also pulling myself together to face my patients. They had their own problems and didn't need to see a "woe is me" face treating them. I arrived before my first patient and went into my private office, closed the door, and sat down at my desk. I took a deep breath to clear my head. Just as the pile of phone messages caught my eye, the phone rang. Carol Goldman, an old friend of mine who I talked with periodically, was calling me about a matter unrelated to Cele's situation. Carol and I enjoyed a casual relationship and enjoyed visiting on the phone, especially after a long period of time had elapsed. We would catch up and exchange news about our kids. Our conversations were typically upbeat and sprinkled with laughter. But not this time.

As we spoke, I couldn't maintain my composure, much less be jovial. I was distraught about the biopsy and couldn't help from breaking down. Carol could hear me crying through my words and had genuine concern for my sadness. She gently asked me what was wrong. It was the first time I said those words out loud. "My mother has inoperable cancer."

Carol was compassionate and offered a powerful thought. She said, in a reassuring enthusiastic voice, "You know, I read this article about Richard Bloch from the H & R Block tax people who used positive thinking to beat his cancer." Carol told me that there were other nontraditional approaches to investigate regarding my mother's treatment before we raised the white flag. Carol surprised me with her positive stance and depth of reassurance. Our relationship had never before led us to such a serious conversation, nor did I know that our philosophies were so much in tune. But I did know I desperately needed to hear her words at that moment. Carol was talking about not giving up, but it was my grandmother's voice that I was hearing. It was like a message from Mimi. That dark velvet box for Cele could wait a good long time.

After we got off the phone, I called my dear friend Joan— "Joni"—Anderson and caught her in the car on the way to a business meeting. At the sound of Joni's voice, I lost it again and starting sobbing. I gave her the news about Cele. Joni felt close to my mother and was deeply upset by the news. She came to my office right after her meeting. When she arrived, we hugged to give each other strength. We cried together for a long time, neither one of us saying a word. We didn't plan or discuss options. We simply consoled each other. Finally, I began to talk. Joni listened as I recounted the morning's events. She reassured me that whatever would happen, she would be there to help me through it. Since I had a patient waiting, we agreed to meet later at my home. All through the rest of that afternoon, Carol's words of encouragement and Joni's support played over and over in my head, giving me a focus that got me through that long day.

By the time Joni drove her car into my driveway that evening, my mind was racing on how to outmaneuver and starve the cancer that was feeding on my mother's very life. Joni is a savvy business lady who, like me, graduated from college later in life and had built a dynamic career within a few years. She had just accepted an executive position at the hospital where I was on staff. Even as we grew in different directions, she in business marketing and journalism and I as a doctor, we always marveled at how our professional paths invariably crossed. Joni was also a loyal friend. We had met through my cousin, Susie, Aunt Marie's daughter. We liked each other from the start and became friends right away. But it wasn't until Mimi had passed away that we became really close. There was a depth and openness to Joni that drew us together. In a way, Joni filled the emotional vacuum my grandmother had left.

We took our usual seats across from each other at my white, square kitchen table. My home was French style, comfortably furnished with everything arranged for easy and harmonious living. One side of the kitchen table was nestled against the wall, leaving room for three chairs. For more than 20 years, Joni and I had made this kitchen our haven—it's where we laughed, cried, gossiped, planned our children's birthday parties, drafted resumes, and wrote news articles. This kitchen was where Mimi and I used to cook up a storm. It was the center of my home where my children grew up, where their friends came over to play because this was a fun house, where we shot lots of home movies, and where Joni and I planned our PTA crusades. We always retreated to the warmth and security of my kitchen to work out our problems. Now, cancer had struck my family again. In all the years Joni and I had been sorting out the stages of our lives over the kitchen table together, we had never dealt with such profound sadness or faced such a monumental challenge as my mother's lung cancer.

After work, I had run by the medical library and picked up books on nutritional approaches to treating illnesses, alternative treatments for cancer, traditional cancer treatments, and current studies on cancer treatments. Before Joni arrived, I had spread my haul and some of my own books all over the kitchen table. Now, after eyeing the table and looking at the large volume of material strewn about, Joni said, "Oh, good, I see you're in action already. That's the Mary Ann I know."

"That's me," I said, feeling that stiff upper lip at work, feeling Mimi watching over me. I was ready to kick cancer in its nasty teeth.

I work fast. Joni moves more slowly and gets the job done

using a steady flow of energy. This difference has worked well between us and for us. I'm certain we were both born with a dominant detective gene. When my daughter Michelle was ill as a child, Joni, an investigative medical reporter at the time, and I sneaked into a private medical library. We were bold. You have to be when it's a matter of life or death. Our undercover investigation had revealed the cause of my daughter's illness, which ultimately led to finding the right physician and facilitating Michelle's recovery. Joni and I were no strangers to the research process.

"We don't have time to waste," I said. "The cancer has advanced so I have to move fast." I've always felt better when I'm busy and never had this been truer than on that night.

While Joni and I were poring over the material on the kitchen table and discussing how we'd approach researching options for "curing" Cele's cancer, the phone rang. It was my son, Randy, calling from college. He knew his "Mamaw"—his pet name for his grandmother—was undergoing a biopsy that day and wanted to know the results. Michelle would call later that evening. At that moment, I was forced to learn how I would answer that question for both Randy and Michelle, who were very close to their grandparents. I'm sure my strong bond with Mimi had rubbed off favorably on my kids.

I didn't have the heart to tell Randy that the doctors gave Mamaw mere months to live. He was alone at college and it wasn't fair to burden him with the news. Instead, I decided to tell him the truth, my truth—a truth that had been buried all day under the weight of what the doctor had told me: "Your mother has two months to live." Cele's death sentence had been handed down, a blind judgment by one of traditional medicine's native sons. Thoughts are like habits that you can pick up from others, some good, some not. The faulty thoughts of others can make you doubt your own instincts and sense of life.

I was determined not to be trapped by the restricted perspective of others. Mimi had unleashed the fighter for positive thinking in me years ago. I had already run the gauntlet of traditional medicine when Michelle had been ill as a child. I had to find my own way to save my daughter then, and I knew I had to find my own way to save my mother now. I was being tested. I wouldn't fail. I simply couldn't. My truth would not be the truth of the establishment and its conventional wisdom. It would be different. It would be mine.

It all came to me in an intuitive flash while Randy was on the phone waiting to hear the news about his Mamaw. I knew precisely what to tell my son. I told him that his grandmother had a cancer that was in a place where the doctors couldn't remove it with surgery and that the best way to treat this particular cancer was with radiation and chemotherapy.

"Grandma will need a lot of help going through the treatments. It'll only last a few months. That's usually how long it takes to kill off the cancer."

I told him that his grandmother was going to feel pretty sick and very weak from these treatments, but that was to be expected. Mamaw might lose her hair, but it would grow back. She would probably lose a lot of weight, but she'll gain that back, too.

I reminded Randy that his other grandfather, his dad's father, had survived cancer twice and was doing fine. Although lung cancer is considered one of the least curable cancers and the doctors offered no hope, I felt secure in telling Randy that his Mamaw had a curable cancer. Was I lying? Is the truth flexible? My truth was on a plateau that you have to feel to know it's rooted in substance. I didn't break down. I didn't cry. I gave Randy the facts as I felt them. I told my son not to worry. I suggested he call his grandmother since she was feeling okay after the biopsy. Although I could have told him more, I knew that hearing his grandmother's voice would answer all his heartfelt questions.

What I didn't know at the time was that the words I spoke to my son, my words of truth, would release a reality that would forever alter our course and send us down a path toward life for my mother. The trick was not to forget the power of that vision as things would most likely get tough.

I could feel myself taking control. Everything was coming naturally into place like a jigsaw puzzle with hundreds of pieces fitting together to form a picture in three-dimensional space.

After I hung up the phone from speaking with Randy, I sat back down at the table with Joni. Her mouth was open but no words came out. Joni was rarely at a loss for words.

"What?" I asked.

All she could say was "Wow!" Finally she could speak. "Do you know what you just did?" she asked.

Again, I asked "What?"

Joni continued. "Well, as we were looking over the books on diet, vitamins and positive thinking that you had scattered on the kitchen table, I admit that, at first, I felt that you were grasping at straws. You know, I use positive thinking in my life all the time. But, I've been asking myself, can these gentle therapies really work against cancer? Cancer is so strong, so virulent. Up against cancer, these treatments sounded like a real stretch, at least for me. I felt cancer was too strong for these methods and I didn't want you to face that cruel disappointment."

"You were worried for me?" I said.

"Yes, but not for long," Joni said. "Because I felt it happen. I felt it in my bones that very moment. I watched you make sense of the whole thing, the big picture, you know?"

"You felt it happen?" I said, still unsure of where Joni was heading.

"Yes, yes, and yes. Your truth became my reality in front of my eyes. I didn't get it right off, but I caught on. I finally realized you had made some kind of quantum shift just now. You were treating the information about cancer as if it were commonplace. Oh, there's nothing to healing cancer. You were talking about it like one of your favorite recipes, and you fully expected to whip up a cure for Cele."

I nodded in the affirmative. Joni was cooking and I was all ears.

"I had private doubts when I came over," Joni continued, "but as I listened to your side of the conversation with Randy, to your tone and clear thinking, my doubts and sadness about Cele lifted off like a balloon. I sat up taller in the kitchen chair and my breathing became more relaxed as you spoke to Randy. It's not only what you said to him, although the words were very positive, but the way you presented it. You didn't see your mother as fighting cancer because that would imply that cancer had a chance to win. Your words struck the tuning fork inside me that hummed the truth."

"How poetic," I said. Joni understood that we define ourselves, our reality, by the words we choose to use. In the end, for better or worse, we all rationalize our actions.

"Well, the truth does seem to bring out poetry," Joni said. "You explained Cele's situation without a charge on it. I'm sure Randy felt the same serene power in your voice just now."

I realized then how important it was to be sharing my truth with Randy, Joni and everyone else, because, for the truth to exist, one must speak it out loud and another must hear it. Only then can the cycle be complete.

"I actually saw Cele getting well," Joni said. "It was going to happen. You laid out the road, brick by brick and I was walking down it with you. Eventually, one-by-one, I knew we would all walk down that road you were building—your mother, your father, Randy, Michelle, your brother Steve, everyone."

"You saw my truth clearly?" I said.

Joni nodded a big yes. "And no matter how bad the news or how difficult the treatments might get, no matter what happened along the way, I knew you had made an unalterable decision. You would never waver from your position. I could almost visualize you laying those bricks that would keep us all moving forward along the path toward wellness."

"Yes, Joni," I said, "sometimes I do feel like Dorothy and the Yellow Brick Road is a mindset leading to health and life."

Joni sat back in her chair looking quite satisfied. "You had no doubts. That's the magic that inspires. I felt it inside."

"I felt it, too," I said. "I believe she will recover from this." This was it. Randy's phone call that night had opened the way for me to crystallize my own feelings, my own plan, for all of us to hear, for me to hear. It was an important moment—perhaps "the" defining moment for my plan to save Mother.

I was heartened by how powerful words can be. Joni had reflected it all back to me. Good friends are like clear mirrors that allow us to see ourselves without the cataracts of self-absorption and ego. If I could change Randy's and Joni's reality, perhaps I could change my mother's as well. The new truth about cancer had germinated in my mind. As with all fragile seedlings, I had to make sure no one stomped it to death with conventional thinking. One day soon I knew my mother would be cancer free with many tomorrows in front of her.

Chapter 12

Ship of Fools

"One does not discover new lands without consenting to lose sight of the shore for a very long time." —Andrè Gide

In contrast to the hush-hush manner in which my family handled Mimi's lung cancer, my mother wasn't kept in the dark. Cele knew she had cancer again. Whenever I was with Mother, I maintained my composure and was very matter-of-fact about her recovery. I reassured her that she'd be well soon by reminding her that she'd beaten cancer once, and she'd do it again.

That was sufficient. I definitely didn't want the specialists filling my mother's head with how much time she had left. I was adamant on that point. Since no one really knows, it made sense to keep one's options open instead of closed. I was no ostrich with her head in the sand. I was fully aware of the grim statistics about lung cancer and the overwhelming mortality rate associated with the disease. I'm no gambler and had no interest in playing the odds. I wanted to have the upper hand and you don't get that by betting against the house. Maybe my mother did have mere months to live. What would I give for the knowledge that would save my mother? What indeed.

If Mimi outlived the doctor's prognosis by two years, my mother could as well—perhaps even longer, much longer. I knew more now. After all, I was a doctor. Until I went to medical school, I hadn't a clue about the gross limitations of medical training in general. Students are taught the current understanding of how the body works as an organic machine. Biology and the mechanics of disease, however, soon take a back seat in the curriculum. Learning to become adept at writing prescriptions becomes a major focus. Prospective doctors must be prepared to write a prescription for every conceivable medical problem that might walk into their office. Medical school emphasizes the importance of naming (diagnosis) a disease or illness and then giving that diagnosis a drug (prescription) to treat it. Surgery is promoted when drugs fail. Diagnosis is, of course, the keystone skill for the profession. Once the problem is identified, proper treatment becomes the primary focus. In this case, the word *proper* is the difference between life or death. I learned early on that not all doctors are created equal. That's it. That's the short form version of medical school training.

Give a mental or physical ache a proper name and you can bill for it. It's the insurance game. In medicine, complementary means in addition to an establishment treatment while alternative refers to a protocol used instead of an establishment treatment. That's why alternative is ironically charged with disparaging comments. "Alternative" steps on the toes of the ingrown infrastructure called the disease business. You have to focus on keeping yourself healthy. Pasteur was only one-half right. He recognized that there were germs and they played a role in illness. That's correct. But he was wrong when he said the germ would cause the disease. The environment your body is in will cause the disease. Germs will alter depending on your body.

Where healing is involved, there are only ways that work. Patients are interested in results, not ideology. That's the big picture and that's the place from which we can see opportunity. Words are powerful. By calling a potentially effective healing method alternative, we place it outside the mainstream and ostracize it's valuable nature.

As any seasoned crime reporter will tell you, if you want to know the truth of a story, follow the money. Doctors who are true healers and can diagnose with compassionate precision are the rare exception in our skewed mainstream system of health care. They do exist. Seek out such doctors. Interview them to make sure they see you as an individual, not a number attached to an HMO claim form. As with all things of great value, it takes work to swim against the mainstream and not drown.

My work with Mother began with this premise: It's what you don't know that can kill you. One of the first things I did after her diagnosis was to research our options. We were already into January 1991, and I had a feeling we were going to come out on top in this new year. Although I had access to one of the finest medical libraries in the country in Fort Worth, my findings were disappointing. I ran a computer search on a Stage III B inoperable, metastatic adenocarcinoma of the lung. There were no options, only article after article spewing out the inevitable prognosis of imminent death from the relentless printer.

Caught up in a grip of terror, I felt frozen in a library chair. There was nothing forthcoming that would give me a shred of hope. I was devastated. Tears began flowing. I couldn't bear it. Was my mother going to die? Optimism, for all its wonderment, is easy prey for the slightest doubt. I was in conflict. I had convinced Randy, Michelle, and Joni that Cele would overcome this disease. And then there was Daddy. Although he never expressed doubts, he never expressed that he was convinced she would live either. He just didn't talk about it, which was his way of dealing with the crisis. I sat at the computer terminal feeling like a fraud. I had sold those dearest to me a bill of goods. And at that moment, it seemed I could never deliver the goods. I was definitely feeling emotionally isolated in the Lone Star State.

Houston, We Have a Problem

There are three basic options they teach you in medical school for treating cancer: chemotherapy, surgery and radiation—sometimes referred to as "poison, slash and burn." Having graduated from an osteopathic medical school, I not only learned how to diagnose and prescribe, I was also taught osteopathic manipulation, a proven concept that introduces noninvasive choices for healing. The osteopathic philosophy states that "The body has an inherent ability to heal itself if given the proper tools to do so." I had an edge. I knew poison, slash and burn were not the only effective tools available to treat my mother. Although osteopathic manipulation wasn't taught as a treatment for cancer when I was a medical student, I would later come to appreciate its power to help Mother with her back pain and sense of well-being.

Timing is everything. I didn't yet know what other healing tools were available; I did know every helpful bit would be significant; I did know that I would have to find these tools if my mother was going to live. I had to determine what her body needed to heal itself. The pressure for answers was intense. When you go out on a limb, be prepared to learn how to fly solo.

Currently, there are 31 regional cancer centers nationwide that meet the tough federal standards for designation as a Comprehensive Cancer Center by the National Cancer Institute. M.D. Anderson at the University of Texas in Houston is one of them. Their focus is exclusively on cancer patient care, education, prevention, and research. M.D. Anderson pioneered the "multidisciplinary" approach to cancer care. Teams of physicians from various disciplines (radiation oncology, medical oncology, and surgery) specialize in treating every kind of cancer. Cele's hometown doctor could only come up with palliative radiation, which might extend her life for a few months. This was a dead end and not good enough.

Going to M.D. Anderson in Houston seemed to be the best next step. It was the closest cancer center and my brother, Steve, lived in Houston. When I called the center, I was informed it would be several weeks before they could see my mother. Several weeks! Mother could be dead by then. This was no time for waiting in line and being patient. Mother had friends who were influential at M.D. Anderson. She called them and they called Houston. Within hours, several weeks had been reduced to an immediate appointment.

According to the medical literature, there was no successful treatment for Cele's type of cancer. But I knew that already. I regrouped and reconsidered as my plan to save Mother developed a life of its own. In addition to the wonderful osteopathic philosophy I had learned and embraced in medical school, I also had access to several exceptional doctors who had become friends and mentors over the years. Before leaving for M.D. Anderson, I called my friend Dr. Bill Jordan, who is an osteopathic physician and an oncologist. I had known Bill since we were in junior high school. He was a caring and excellent physician, that rare breed of doctor I had mentioned earlier. He was a straight-shooter and this was Texas. I told him about my mother's plight and that we were headed for the cancer institute. Bill didn't discourage me from taking her to M.D. Anderson. After all, he had trained at that center himself.

Bill did prophetically advise me: "When they tell you there's nothing they can do for her except palliative radiation, come on back here. I have a protocol that's showing some success." Palliative, in this case, meant a treatment that can slow the spread of the cancer, not halt the growth or effect a cure. Palliative radiation might increase Mother's life to six months—Cele's primary physician had already informed us about that short road. But when you're dying, you stretch further than you thought possible, hoping to grab the brass ring.

Daddy, Mother and I drove to Love Field in Dallas for our flight to Houston. As the airplane lifted off the ground, I could hear the landing gear retract. We were airborne. We had begun and that was the hardest part. The die was cast and I was bursting with hope.

After landing in Houston, we went directly to my brother's house. Steve and his family were great and did their best to be as helpful as possible. It would have been difficult for Mother if we had to check into a hotel, which was impersonal and lacked the conveniences of a house. Although staying with my brother made it easier on Mother, it wasn't home, which is where you want to be when you're ill and feeling vulnerable. It's awkward enough to be a houseguest when you're visiting. Now, it was palpably stressful that Cele was fearful for her life. We were all scared. Despite the tension, our conversations for the rest of day and evening were light. Mother and Daddy slept in my nieces' room, since the twins were off at college, while I made my bed on the sofa in the den. That night, I tried to think of all the positive things in my life. I thought of my children. Like their cousins, Michelle and Randy were also away at college, preparing for their future. All in all, I was a lucky person. Things would work out, I thought, as I turned out the light.

The next morning, we drove to M.D. Anderson, which lies south of downtown Houston in the University of Texas Medical Center. Nothing much was said during our drive. We were kept busy looking for the right streets and where to park once we had arrived. Like the image of most things in Texas, the M.D. Anderson Center was a huge, imposing building made of glass and brick. Its massive curved architectural style had a timeless feel. From the exterior view, the building could have been built in 1940 or yesterday. I was pleased to see that the entire grounds, including the parking lot, was a nonsmoking area. I thought, would we find the wizard who would save Mother inside?

After we went through the tedious formalities of checking Cele in, she was assigned to a physician who would manage her case during her stay at the center. We met her doctor, an older gentleman, in his office. They brought in an extra chair for me and we all sat there together. The doctor had been in the cancer field for many years and he couldn't have been nicer or more accommodating. He was cordial and acted as if he had nothing else to do all day but talk to us and make us feel comfortable. I waited for a private moment, then pulled the doctor aside. I told him that I wanted no one to tell my mother how much time she had left.

He smiled knowingly and said, "I'll be retiring soon. The one thing I've learned after being in this field for many, many, years is that no one knows how long someone else will live. As soon as I tell someone they have two months to live they'll turn around and live thirty more years. And if I told a patient that they were 'cured' they might die the next day. I've learned that in this business, it's best to never tell someone how long they have to live."

This was music to my ears. I was greatly relieved and knew this doctor and I would get along. He was kind and thoughtful. When he found out that I was an osteopathic physician, he immediately brought in a young woman who was on a fellowship at the center. She turned out to be a graduate of my alma mater, the Texas College of Osteopathic Medicine. We had actually met when I was in school and she was doing her residency at the hospital where I did rotations. She was helpful, enthusiastic, and on call to answer any questions if Mother's doctor was not available.

We spent nearly two harrowing weeks at M.D. Anderson. Mother had all kinds of tests: X rays, CT scans, and blood work.

Cele saw many different doctors. Was there a physician at the center who had enough experience and technological finesse with this kind of cancer to surgically remove it? No one at home was willing to risk it. We just hoped that since they did so many surgeries, someone at the center might have the skill to pull it off. If no one could surgically remove the tumor, perhaps the hospital had a cutting-edge treatment protocol that would successfully kill the cancer growing inside my mother's chest. Either way, I wanted someone to tell me that it could be fixed, and that my mother would live.

Days were spent sitting, waiting between tests, and seeing different doctors. Although it was a stressful time for all of us, she was the one waiting to find out if she was going to live or not. One late afternoon, as we were walking toward the parking lot at the end of one of those interminable days at the hospital, my mother, looking exhausted, broke down and cried, which was entirely out of character for her. Never one for sitting around, Mother was tired of all the waiting. The ordeal was finally getting to her. At least, that was my assessment.

Like Mimi, Cele always handled anything that came along with a composed strength. But perhaps she had made it her business to appear strong in front of me. Although I don't recall the circumstances, I clearly remember seeing Mother cry only a couple of times in my life. Her tears triggered a terror that was constantly dwelling within me. I was afraid my courage had really been false bravado. I was afraid I was going to lose my mother. I kept my doubts and terror to myself. I hugged my sobbing mother, hoping my arms would bring her some comfort. By the time we got in the car, Mother had regained her usual bearing. We drove back to my brother's home.

A Ship to Nowhere

Spending your days in a cancer hospital can be depressing, which is a big understatement. Even if you're the fortunate one who doesn't have cancer, walking around the center, seeing all those who do, can get to you after a while. Like some fantastic surrealistic vision, many patients were ambling about holding on to IV poles on wheels. From the poles hung clear plastic tubing with chemicals dripping into their arms. Other souls, who had lost all of their hair and most of their weight, looked as if they were victims of the Nazi Holocaust.

The M.D. Anderson complex had many different areas for treatment. They also had rooms just to pass the time. There was a library and a game room available for the patients. After one of Mother's exams, we all sat in the game room. I tried taking our minds away from this place. "Let's pretend," I said to my parents, "that we're on a cruise ship sailing off to an exotic port of call and we've run into a storm at sea." Since they loved to travel, a voyage of the imagination seemed a good choice to escape our true surroundings. We could read in the ship's library or entertain ourselves with such diversions as scrabble, cards, or jigsaw puzzles in the game room. Although I don't think my role-playing gambit fooled anyone, Mother and Daddy went along. Sometimes you have to act brave to be brave. Time passed with a little less stress and my cruise scenario seemed to hold grim reality at bay.

Lab Rats Only

After Cele had been poked and prodded for nearly a fortnight, we met with her doctor again in his office. As we sat waiting to hear about a miracle, some late-breaking news, I felt the icy cold in the air. I could tell from the doctor's face, rigid body language, and ultimately his tentative words, where this conversation was going. To his credit, he didn't start with "I'm sorry." He explained what we already knew. The position of the tumor in the mediastinal area would soon impinge upon vital vessels and organs. In the end, he agreed with her doctor in Fort Worth. Surgery would be too dangerous. Mother wouldn't survive. If it wasn't so painful, I could almost have laughed at the slightly altered old saw: The operation would be a success, but the patient would die. They could offer her palliative radiation only, which might help shrink the tumor and buy her a little time. But precious time had already been spent and now we were back at square one. I could hear Dr. Bill Jordan's voice. His prediction fit the frustrating outcome to the letter.

The doctor didn't cross the life prediction line—he had kept his word. But I already knew what he really thought. A few days earlier, while Cele was getting some blood drawn, he took me aside and spoke to me doctor to doctor, saying, "She probably has no more than two months to live, maybe six months even with palliative radiation."

As the three of us sat in the doctor's office for our final meeting with him, I didn't much feel like a physician who had set up her private practice a few months earlier. Dwarfed by the cancer that had invaded our lives, years of medical training seemed to have vanished. Here and now, I was Cele's loving daughter—no more, no less.

At any given time, M.D. Anderson has about 700 clinical trials in progress. Physicians conduct clinical studies hoping to establish new treatments that will be as good as or better than the current standard care. Patients in a study treatment are among the first to benefit from these clinical therapies—that is, if they work at all.

"What about other protocols?" I said. "Surely M.D. Anderson has other treatments for lung cancer besides palliative radiation!"

"Of course we do," he said. "But things are not so simple. We're dealing with a bureaucracy and strict guidelines for everything. Because your mother had another cancer ten years ago, she can't enter any of our other treatment protocols. I'm sorry."

I could not believe my ears. "Why? What did one cancer have to do with the other?" I said, feeling like an exposed raw nerve.

He explained in a quiet voice that M.D. Anderson is a research center. The subjects they accept must fall into a certain category. If one doesn't fit the criteria, then that subject cannot participate. It's that cut-and-dried. Policy over humanity was once again rearing its ugly head. Until that moment, I had no idea M.D. Anderson was so restrictive and limited to treating people exclusively under research protocols. No one had ever mentioned this policy to me before our stay. Perhaps the center's medical form had spelled it out, but I didn't notice it. We came to M.D. Anderson hoping they would either be able to perform the risky surgery that local doctors wouldn't attempt or that they had some new trial that might be successful for Mother. When you're in fear of losing a loved one, the fine print can get away from you. You want to see what you believe. I have learned since that many people who go there to this very day don't know about the center's policy either.

I was distraught. Even though there might have been a treatment going on in a nearby room somewhere in the center that could help my mother, she wouldn't receive it because she didn't fit into an acceptable research category. The red tape was exasperating. No one at the center was forthcoming with viable alternatives. No one told us that there might be other doctors conducting research in private practice who were not tied to these strict guidelines and might be able to help us.

The doctor restated that the center could only provide

palliative radiation for Mother at this time. There was nothing left to say. He excused himself and left the office. In the silence, I could hear my heart pounding like a fist against reality. Mother, Daddy and I were alone on many levels. After hearing this frustrating and devastating news, I barely held back the tears. If I looked defeated, I knew Mother would feel defeated. I turned away to leave the room before my mother and father could see me crying. I was overwhelmed with a profound fear and sadness. As my parents followed behind me like loyal and trusting puppies, I willed myself back into composure and wiped the tears from my cheeks. With all the assurance and confidence that a daughter could muster, I turned to my mother, who was now standing in front of me, and looked her right in the eye.

"Well, it's all up to you now," I said.

With the stiff upper lip I knew so well, Cele, exhausted and worn down, still managed a nod of agreement. If my mother was going to survive, she'd have to fight and I'd have to be her trainer, manager and cheerleader. We went to Houston and we still had a problem.

Doctor Jordan, here we come.

Chapter 13

Back to Our Future

"Mother Love is the fuel that enables a normal human being to do the impossible." —Unknown

On February 6, 1991, Mother, Daddy, and I left the imposing and now oddly impotent M.D. Anderson building behind us. It was a late morning—overcast, looking like rain. We, too, felt downcast. We left the building that had promised so much from a distance and offered nothing once inside. We left the center with all its tests, protocols, inflexible clinical studies, and false hope. Though I might have been justified in feeling hopeless, I knew better. I knew this down feeling would pass. I knew I had to try everything. This was part of the grand plan. To know in your heart that you did all you possibly could is character and salvation.

As I drove my mother and father back to my brother's house, traffic whizzed past us. Everyone seemed to be rushing to get somewhere, in a hurry to reach the destinations in their lives. Each car contained people and each person contained a story. We usually don't stop to consider the trials and tribulations of others. In this respect, we might as well be on different planets or, as Mimi might have put it, on "Another World"—her favorite soap opera. How were my fellow travelers faring on the highway? It was an ordinary day for most; an extraordinary day for some; and a devastating day for those whose hopes were vanishing before their eyes. We weren't the only family jumping through hoops in Hades, yet it felt as if we were. Here we are, I thought, in the city that was mission control for landing a man on the moon in 1969—one of the historic moments in my lifetime. If NASA could do the impossible, maybe saving my mother was also in the realm of the doable. Yes, that was it. People need to get used to the impossible before it can be achieved. You have to overcome the limitation hurdle bound by old thoughts before new standards are set. Yes, I thought, the eagle can definitely land again in the Sea of Tranquillity, with Mother along for the ride.

I did my best to remain upbeat when I gave Steve and his wife, Gail, the news that we had struck out at the center. Everyone did his and her best to support Cele. We tried reassuring her and ourselves that all would still be okay. It wasn't the end of the world. We'd find another way. Cele would get through this in good shape. We packed our bags and, with heavy hearts, headed off to the airport. This was surely the worst day of my life.

During our flight home, we sat across in a row—Daddy on the aisle, Mother in the middle, and me at the window. I was determined to keep our spirits up, including my own. I kept the conversation going about this and that so Mother wouldn't dwell on the harsh disappointment. After the "no hope" news her doctor at M.D. Anderson had told me, clinging to that smooth-as-glass, rose-colored wall called denial was leaving me with bloodied fingernails. I couldn't allow myself to think this cancer could kill my mother. Still, unless I could find a way to change her prognosis, I knew she would die. I would not give up on Mother, or myself.

As we flew over Texas, I reminded Mother that my friend, Dr. Bill Jordan, said he had a protocol that was getting great results. He never actually used the word "great," but she didn't need to know I was exercising a bit of poetic healing license. Mother needed to hear that there was hope. Although her doctor at M.D. Anderson hadn't told her how much time she had left, he hadn't offered any hope either. Mother needed to believe she could survive and that she would survive. But there is a distinction between survival and cure. Conventional medicine says "cure" if the patient has survived five years beyond the initial diagnosis. Cure, in truth, means that the patient is completely free and clear of the disease—now and forever.

While at the center, Cele systematically asked every doctor she met if anyone had ever survived her type of lung cancer. I was relieved she didn't use the word "cure." Fortunately, all the doctors had said: "Yes." Mother would then come back with: "Very good. If one person has survived, then I will, too." These were our straws of hope blowing about, back and forth, in the fickle wind called uncertainty. When you're dying, you want to believe there is hope, and with hope you create your world and the opportunity to find your miracles. There's a danger here, however. Hope can be a treacherous state of mind if its companion, action, isn't present to transform anticipation into a desired reality.

The jet engines moaned and droned. I was exhausted from the stress. I looked over at my dear mother. She was sitting there as if in a daze, which was understandable. Cele had just gone through an awful two weeks and you wouldn't know it from her lips. She didn't complain. She was a fighter, a partisan for life. Things suddenly got quiet inside my head. As the plane whisked us through the sky, I sat back and drew in a deep breath. Slowly and effortlessly, my head streamed with bits and pieces of memories about my mother.

I was a bashful little girl. Although Mimi told me she had been a shy child, too, I could never believe it. My grandmother was a splendid extrovert, a natural born friendly person. She would stop and talk to everybody. She was the mayor of all that she surveyed; she could have gone far in politics. After she died, our appreciation of her soared even further as we received condolence letters from people far and wide. Mimi treated everyone with respect, a wave, and a smile—a simple, yet powerful formula for making friends and having a positive effect on people.

My mother had told me that she had been shy as a young girl, too. I would have hardly chosen "shy" to describe my mother. While not quite as outgoing as Mimi, she was no wallflower. Both women admitted they had been shy when they were young and that they had managed to grow out of it. Mother knew how to deal with my shyness in a supportive, yet firm manner. When I was 6-years-old, I didn't want to attend Sunday school. I was timid, and for no particular reason I could think of. Cele was outrageously creative, especially when it came to her family. By being nearby only if I needed her, she figured out how to be my security blanket without smothering me or my development. Somehow, she became the Sunday school teacher and that made me feel great.

Cele used the same strategy when I started kindergarten. She became my room mother, which involved helping out in the classroom, planning school parties, and attending field trips. If there was something I couldn't handle, she was there to handle it, or help me manage the situation myself. It might sound as if Mother was running too much interference for me. Not so. Mother knew precisely what she was doing. Cele was my Mary Poppins—a little bit of sugar did make the medicine go down. By balancing the fine line of doing things for me with being there in the wings until I could do them myself, Mother taught me to toughen up—a quality needed to get through difficult times, which is how it's done in nature.

I knew my mother was there for me. It was a given, something I could count on forever. I knew she would pick me up if I fell. How do you encourage independence in a child, especially a shy one? Pushing them out of the nest prematurely can have the opposite effect of increasing dependency. Coddling them isn't the answer either. Being there for them until they're ready promotes an indelible form of independence. Certainly, the "until they're ready" part is a judgment call. That's why there is an art to parenting and my mother was a master.

Cele knew before I did when it was time for me to leave the nest. When I was a young adult, she realized I needed to find a direction in life. It was all very matter-of-fact to Cele and she transferred this can-do attitude to me—as Mimi had done with her. Mother felt I was limiting my life by living at home. I had a nothing dead-end job as I hadn't finished college. My social life wasn't thriving either. In the late '60s, Fort Worth had a very limited young singles group of people. She sensed I was ready for an adventure.

"Mary Ann," she said, "I love you. You've got to do something with your life. For starters, you need to be off on your own and see what that's all about."

She thought I would learn about independence and have more fun living in a big city like Houston or Denver. I chose Houston where I still had many friends from my college days. One of them introduced me to someone who was looking for a roommate. I went down with enough money to last 6 months without a job. I knew I had a safe haven if I ever needed to return home. Fortunately, I found a good job pretty quickly.

It was probably harder for Cele to have me leave than it was for me to move to another city. But she knew I needed to evolve and it wasn't happening on our cozy home turf. Mother knew that in this tough world, every living thing can end up as lunch for some other living thing. She wanted me to be prepared for whatever came up. At the time, it would have been much easier for us both if only we had been clairvoyant. On one of my visits back home to Fort Worth, Carol Goldman would fix me up on my predestined blind date to meet Stan. This was the same Carol who had called me at my office out of the blue with encouraging words the day Mother was diagnosed with lung cancer. Two years after meeting Stan, I would return from Houston to Fort Worth as Mary Ann Block, a married woman.

Then, again, if we knew what was to be, what would be the point?

Roots and Wings

There is a saying I like that embodies the essence of my mother: "There are two gifts you can give your children—one is roots, the other is wings." The roots were always there if I needed them. At the same time, she encouraged me to sprout wings and fly. If my mother thought my leaving home was a good idea, then I'd do it. Her confidence in me made me bold; Mother's trust in me had made all the difference.

As a young child, you might say I led an enchanted life. I wanted for nothing. Mother and Daddy didn't burden me with the troubles of the adult world. They were protecting me with a discriminating intelligence that allowed me to flourish at my own pace without being isolated from reality. Mother was a fabulous cook. Each meal was terrific. She could take one chicken and turn it into two meals for our family of four and still have chicken soup left over. She swore she liked the wings of the chicken best. How did I know she was saving the meaty parts for the rest of us? Mother put her love where her mouth was.

Cele's Haute Couture

In addition to being shy, I was tiny for my age. I was 13 but looked about 9, or younger. For me to have clothes that fit and still look like they were made for a teenager, my mother decided to master dressmaking. Cele was the mother of invention. She didn't sew from a pattern either; she made her own. She was talented and resourceful. Her abilities would surface in wonderful and unexpected ways. This was our modus operandi, or M.O.: first we would go shopping. Then when I found a dress, skirt, or some article of clothing I liked, she'd pull out a small pad and pencil and quickly sketch it on the fly. Finally, with blueprint in hand, Mother and I, like two secret agents, would rush home where she would go to work.

In a day or so later, she'd dress me in one of her marvelous creations. I had a hand-tailored wardrobe of all the latest styles that were fit for a princess. Mother felt details were important, so much so that she made an extra effort. She would even remove authentic manufacturers' labels from her clothes and sew them inside the clothing she had made for me. No one could tell they weren't store-bought, off-the-rack clothing. It didn't matter to me if others knew my mother made my clothes. I didn't see it as a negative. I was proud that my mother cared so much about my appearance and how I felt. I wore these special clothes with pride and dignity. I had great clothes that fit, loving parents, a decent older brother, and I was beginning to feel a lot less shy. Life was almost perfect, except for one thing: I wet the bed.

Like Mimi, Mother knew the mind was a powerful resource. Positive thinking kept us healthy; negative thinking made us sick. The metaphysical math was simple and irrefutable. I was a bed wetter. Who knows why? Lots of kids go through this childhood problem and they usually grow out of it. I was still wetting the bed when I was 15. My mother was patient. No histrionics over another soiled sheet. No trauma to the little bed wetter. I never received a scolding or was made to feel bad in any way about peeing in bed. I was feeling pretty ashamed about it all on my own.

One day Mother confided in me. "Mary Ann, you don't have to worry. Wetting the bed tends to run in the family. And we all turned out just fine." She told me matter-of-factly that both she and Daddy had both been bed wetters when they were kids and it was nothing to be embarrassed about. Knowing this new information did help me feel better but it didn't stop me from wetting my bed.

Mother knew I was still frustrated and was looking for ways to solve my problem. At one point, Mother brought me a book and said: "Read this and see if it helps." It was *The Power of Positive Thinking* by Norman Vincent Peale. In his classic book, Peale outlined how one could accomplish goals through positive thinking. Peale's down-to-earth manner gave many easy-to-understand examples of how the power of thought worked in our daily lives—for good, or not. His words and philosophy sounded just like my mother, just like Mimi. Every night before I went to bed, I would stand in front of the mirror. I would look myself in the eye and say: "Tonight, I will not wet the bed. Tonight, I will not wet the bed." I didn't think the words or mouth the words. I said them out loud, over and over again until I felt within my heart that it was true. One night, Mother had come into my bedroom and caught me talking to myself in the mirror. I felt embarrassed and quickly clammed up. Cele gave me her smile of approval and quietly backed out of the room without saying a word. I did my mirror talk for several consecutive weeks and, to my amazement, it worked. I stopped wetting the bed. I had grown up. Although Mother and Daddy were pleased for me, they didn't make a fuss about my stopping as they hadn't made a big deal about wetting the bed in the first place. They were consistent and that had a great impact on my growing up strong.

Suddenly, I felt a bit of a jolt. The jet engines were cutting back. We were slowing and descending on our approach flight path into Love Field. I looked over at Cele. She had already fixed herself up with fresh lipstick and Daddy's face tried hard not to fall into a somber mask. Yes, I thought, that's my mother. She gave me the gift of her motherhood. She made it clear that mothering is a proud profession, a calling. She taught me by example that if you're going to be a parent, it's the most important job you can have. She taught me that you do whatever you have to do for your children. This is what she did for me and I could do no less for her. Having grown children of my own, I also knew how difficult it is to walk that fine line between roots and wings. Cele had set an admirable standard. She was my role model for parenting.

"Mother," I said, emphatically.

"Yes," she said, sounding a bit alarmed.

"Remember that self-help book you gave me when I was a bed wetter?"

She laughed. "Sure do. As I recall, we had dry nights soon after."

"I still have that book and I feel it should be yours now," I said.

She understood immediately and gave me a knowing smile as the plane touched down.

We were back home and the clock was ticking.

Chapter 14

Any Port in a Storm

*"The enemy has made the most skilled generals of medicine run
up the white flag of surrender."* —Andrew T. Still, MD

O ur hardest work was ahead of us. I had to find a way to cure
my mother and she had to succeed at doing it. Time was a
luxury that we didn't have. I was determined to study every
treatment I could find. Despite the billions of dollars being
spent on research, cancer was still winning. The imminent
breakthrough, the cure, remained forever pregnant with no delivery date in sight. Once you actually study the disease, you
begin to see it in a new light. The real question about cancer is
not why do some people get it, but why doesn't everyone get it.
There was no answer. I could tell the doctors were giving us
their best-guess answers. I didn't want guesswork. I wanted my
mother to live.

I thought the whole thing out as dispassionately as possible.
Our plan had to be focused and flexible. I felt like a field general. It didn't matter if the treatment belonged to one of the
"poison, slash, or burn" categories or some other treatment. I
would use anything that anyone had tried with positive results.
I didn't care if the treatment had been tested on a thousand
people, or used successfully on one patient. It didn't matter if
the treatment had been "published in the medical literature" or

not. If it might help and wouldn't hurt, we were going to try it. Everyone needs a champion. I was going to be this champion for Cele.

Radiation and Chemotherapy

My first move was clear. Going to M.D. Anderson had been a necessary detour. We had to establish that traditional medical protocols alone wouldn't save my mother. As soon as I got home from the airport, I made an appointment for Mother with my friend, Dr. Bill Jordan, and his associate, Dr. Greg Friess, another oncologist who had been one of my professors in medical school. After examining Mother, both doctors felt she was a candidate for their therapy, which included chemotherapy and radiation for several months. Mother was relieved, if that was possible, to know she'd be receiving traditional treatment at home instead of being isolated in another city and confined to a depressing medical center. At least she'd be in her own home and near her friends. If she was going to be sick, she would much rather face the music from her own bed.

It was Dr. Friess who had developed the chemotherapy and radiation treatment that Dr. Jordan had told me about before our pilgrimage to M.D. Anderson. Friess and Jordan were getting better results with this treatment than radiation or chemotherapy alone. At the time, palliative radiation was the only official treatment—as we learned the hard way. No one else was combining radiation and chemotherapy together for this type of lung cancer. At least these doctors were willing to try something new.

Chemotherapy, or the use of chemical agents to destroy cancer cells, is a mainstay in the treatment of malignancies. I knew chemotherapy had a limited success range of 2 to 5 percent. I

was dealing with dreams, not odds. I wouldn't get trapped into thinking about how things didn't work. I did know that chemotherapy could decrease tumor size, but that wasn't to be confused with getting rid of the cancer. I also knew that a major advantage of chemotherapy is its ability to treat widespread or metastatic cancer, whereas surgery and radiation therapies are limited to treating cancers that are confined to specific areas.

Burn and poison wasn't going to be a walk-through for Cele by any stretch of the imagination. It was going to be a rough and bumpy ride. For starters, Mother would receive the chemotherapy through a surgically implanted plastic port in her chest. Before my mother began chemotherapy, her doctors drew some blood. Her white blood cell count was already on the low side. The white blood cell population indicates how well the immune system is working, or not. Significant numbers of her white cells would most likely be destroyed by the chemotherapy. The ravages of radiation poisoning wouldn't become apparent during the treatment phase. But the aftermath was another story. Radiation burns would leave her with fibrosis of the lungs, causing her to develop breathing problems and asthma-like symptoms. Another radiation aftershock would cause osteoporosis in her vertebrae. Living through this invasion would test Cele's body and faith. Could I hold together inside and visualize my reality long enough for my mother to survive? We were facing, up close and personal, that old universal truism—solve one problem, and several more shoot up like weeds to take its place.

A few years earlier, Dr. Friess had published a paper on his radiation and chemotherapy treatment that included the history of one patient, a woman, that immediately gave me an intravenous jolt of hope. Although her cancer hadn't been eliminated, this patient was still alive five years after being diagnosed with terminal lung cancer. For this type of cancer, being alive after five years was nothing short of a miracle. If the protocol had already helped one person, then maybe Mother could live

for five more years, too—at the very least. When it came to my mother living longer, I was greedy.

Another factor that made a huge difference in my mother's new treatment program was the attitude of her doctors. They didn't have a chip on their shoulders. Although Drs. Jordan and Friess were unfamiliar with the alternative treatments I was gathering in my campaign, they were supportive of my plan to utilize whatever could possibly work. Whether they believed that any of the alternative treatments would be helpful or not was not an issue with either of them. They didn't discourage me from trying them, which is what any good physician should do. Both Mother and I respected them. That was important. It takes guts to break from the pack of tired convention. So, what we had here were supportive doctors employing a spin on traditional protocols. It was better than nothing.

Cele didn't need to know that only one person had survived Dr. Friess's treatment, or that this person still had cancer. Sometimes not knowing does help—an exception to my don't tell rule for Cele. If a doctor tells a patient that they're going to die in twelve months, you can be sure the patient will oblige and die as scheduled. I'd seen that drill and knew the mechanism. Mother needed to hear she was going live, not die. It was that simple. It was a matter of discretion. Mother believed the chemotherapy and radiation would kill her cancer. Mother's belief that the invasive therapy would help bring her life back kept her from falling apart. I had goals for her. I wanted her to live in my reality where she would be cancer-free. To hear that someone else had survived the same type of cancer was the only important thing for her to know at the time. My mother will not learn about my selective truth telling of her treatment until she reads this book.

Because of her doctors' schedules, Mother saw more of Dr. Friess during her treatment phase. She found him to be as kind and caring as Dr. Jordan. Whenever I called Dr. Friess to find

out how my mother was doing, he was consistently supportive and patient with me. Mother soon became fond of both doctors. She told me and many of her friends more than once that, "Those are the nicest and best doctors I have ever seen."

Whose Illness Is This?

In the pursuit of getting my mother well, I found several books that dealt with alternative healing treatments and positive affirmations for her to read. When I brought them to her house, she said, "Mary Ann, please read them for me and tell me what they say. Tell me what I need to do and I'll do it."

I said, "No, this is your illness, Mother. You have to read the books yourself and decide which things make sense to you and which things you choose to do that will help you overcome the cancer."

It wouldn't do any good for me to tell Mother what the books recommended. She had to embrace her own treatment. She had to believe and trust that whatever she was doing would work. If I believed in a particular approach and she didn't, then the power of thought would be in the wrong head. The cancer would end up winning—even though I wanted to think the disease didn't have a chance. If I believed in a treatment, I knew that she would more likely accept it. But I knew my endorsement alone wouldn't be good enough. Cele had to decide for herself; she had to feel it was right for herself. I could pave the way for her, laying down and building the path brick by brick as my friend, Joni, had described to me so poetically. I could teach Mother everything I knew but ultimately it was her journey. She had to walk the walk. She was the only one who could get herself well.

Next, I focused on Mother's diet. Mother had a sweet tooth

and loved her candy, especially chocolate. I told her she needed to cut sugar from her diet. I showed her an article that explained how sugar can considerably weaken the immune system. I could feel Cele resisting. I knew giving up sweets wasn't going to be easy for her. When you're dying, you don't want to give up the things that do make you feel good. She also had to start eating vegetables. Mother told me she never really liked vegetables, which was a shock to me. Mother's cooking had always been excellent and well-balanced when I was a child. Great vegetables were part of our dinners. I grew up loving vegetables, unaware that Mother wasn't eating them. As I mentioned earlier, I also thought Mother loved chicken wings, only to learn much later that she saved the tasty fleshy morsels for the rest of the family. I didn't know everything about my mother as a kid or now as an adult helping her fight for her life. I was sure learning fast as the enemy brought us closer together with each passing day.

"Mother," I said. "The time for change is now. This is about what you need to do, not what you would like to do. You must say no to sugar and yes to vegetables." I knew Mother understood it all. After all, she had taught me that you've got to do what you've got to do for your children. Only now, the roles were reversed.

Mother nodded her head in silent agreement—as if to say, O.K., bring on the broccoli, the Brussels sprouts, the green beans, and the whole lot of them. Once Mother made up her mind, I could count on her to follow through. Anything that would give her an edge would boost the effectiveness of the total protocol program for saving her life. If one person could survive, so could Mother. That thought became my pulse. It was like the first time a runner had broken the four-minute mile nearly fifty years ago. After that barrier had been broken, other runners began doing the mile in under four minutes. Soon, the impossible had become the expectation. This was the impossible barrier perception that I had been thinking about. You have to get used to the impossible to make it a reality. Trailblazers make it possible for others to reach goals that had been previously thought unattainable. Mother would have to do the metaphorical four-minute mile. Fortunately, it had already been done by the woman survivor in Dr. Friess's clinical study.

Any Which Way You Can

When I began plotting Mother's campaign against the cancer, I had only been practicing medicine for a few months. I didn't treat cancer patients and hadn't planned on starting. Circumstances, however, put me in the position of needing to know everything I could learn about beating the cancer that was eating its way through my mother's lungs. Becoming an expert or specialist isn't complicated. All it takes is the motivation to work hard and find out everything you can. There's no one stopping anyone from becoming an expert in any field. Opportunity is always ripe for truly inquiring minds.

I had several doctor friends from medical school who had made it their practice to be on the cutting edge of treating different medical problems. Their protocols included a variety of alternative options for improving the immune system—which, in turn, would help the body resist and overcome disease. Number one on my list of experts was Dr. George Juetersonke. He was a good friend and one of my primary mentors in medical school. Dr. Juetersonke taught Preventive Medicine and Public Health at Texas College of Osteopathic Medicine. When I was a medical student, I spent my compulsory rotation time with Dr. Juetersonke. During that month of on-the-job training, I was his shadow as he treated patient after patient in his busy office at the school. Not only was he a compassionate physician, he was also a brilliant man. I knew I could learn a lot from watching him, and I did. After all, you've got to spend time with someone if you want to know who they are and what makes them tick.

After I graduated, we continued to keep in touch. Later on, Dr. Juetersonke moved to Colorado Springs, Colorado. Anytime I had a question, I knew he was good for meaningful input. We were definitely connected. It was uncanny. I'd call him up about something and he'd tell me that he had just been reading up on that very topic—which would give me goose bumps. To back up his claim, he'd send me one or more excellent medical articles on the subject.

When I called Dr. Juetersonke about my mother's condition, it felt as if he'd been waiting for my call. We did have a special connection. He dived right in and recommended a program of nutrition, vitamins, and medications to assist her immune system in fighting the cancer. To one degree or another, these were things I was doing. I was already on track. He also enlightened me about a biopharmacotherapy program he'd read about that utilized biological materials to arouse the immune system into action. Instead of attacking the localized symptom of the disease such as a tumor with poison, slash, or burn, this experimental protocol would enhance the body's own innate ability to cure itself (for information about this program, see Part Two of this book).

In his wonderfully predictable pattern, Dr. Juetersonke immediately sent me the biopharmacotherapy protocol, and I went to work. Some elements of the therapy program were unavailable or difficult to procure, such as a specially killed staph vaccine used to stimulate and strengthen the immune system. We began with whatever we could obtain, keeping in mind that something was better than nothing. Since I had only been practicing medicine for a short while and I certainly didn't believe I could be wholly objective when it came to my mother's health care, I enlisted the aid of several other doctors who helped administer the protocol.

The fragments and sum total of Cele's cancer protocol were coming together—a bit of this and a bit of that, whatever had worked and wouldn't hurt—or, at least, wouldn't kill her right off. Poison and burn were invasive to the body and definitely not user-friendly treatments. I kept my eye on the big picture. We were assembling the most effective healing treatments from both the conventional and complementary camps.

About the same time Mother began her chemotherapy and radiation, I took her to a local health food shop in Fort Worth. I knew the owner was knowledgeable and informed on the subject of supplements.

The shop owner was under a lot of pressure. The FDA was trying to limit the sale of certain nutritional supplements. Back in the late '80s and early '90s, the FDA was using Texas as an example. Health food stores in Texas were under particular scrutiny. If a health food store employee told a customer that a specific supplement on the FDA "hit list" would help or combat a particular disease, the health food store could be closed and all of its products confiscated. Whether this story was factual or not, health food store owners thought it was true and were scared to say much of anything to their customers.

Fortunately, this owner knew me well enough to know that I wasn't wearing a wire as a spy for the FDA. As the three of us walked down the aisles stocked with rows of vitamins and supplements, he told me that it was against the law for him to recommend or even imply that any particular nutrient would help my mother. But through eye contact and innuendo, our astute proprietor let me know which products could help fight the cancer. We followed him and began placing a variety of vitamins, minerals and other nutritional supplements in my basket (see Part Two of this book for information about these supplements).

I was grateful to the store owner for helping us. We left the health food shop feeling more powerful. We were operating out of hope supported with action. We were bringing in reinforcements for our campaign to eliminate the disease. We were mounting an all-out offensive. Our healing camp was rallying and burning torches of light for Mother.

Chapter 15

If You Can Visualize It, You Can Attain It

"Listen to the sounds of sea gulls as ocean waves pound the surf. Close your eyes and remain at peace. Let the whole of your body relax and listen very carefully. If you feel like sleeping, go to sleep. In fact, it would be a good idea if you do go to sleep.

Go to sleep and continue sleeping. The deeper your sleep, the better you will perceive and remember everything that I am telling you. You will then be able to listen in harmony, and will therefore go into a deep and sound sleep.

Let your body be completely relaxed, peaceful, and free from any distractions—and accept with pleasure the positive suggestions which you are now receiving. A cosmic energy is always flowing into your body and system, and everything I am telling you will remain in your memory, your subconscious and unconscious minds. And these positive suggestions are going to benefit your body and your life.

Consciously or unconsciously, your whole system is going to be bathed by positive suggestions.

Tonight and every night, your sleep is going to be peaceful, silent, calm, deep and happy. Nothing is going to disturb you. And every time you wake up you will notice a wonderful feeling of re-laxation and well-being. Your blood circulation from now on and always will be fluid and regenerating. You are going to feel good, very happy—and with a lot of desire to live.

The cosmic energy you are always will be transformed into a new vigor and vitality which will rejuvenate your system. You will never suffer depression as other people may, and there will be no reason to worry. That impatience and that anxiety will be a thing of the past. You will not fear anything and will always be at peace.

And each time you wake up, you will have a sensation of well-being, happiness, and joy. Remember, you will be very happy and joyful. All the fears, worries, anxieties, and adversities that can disturb you will have magically disappeared forever.

Pay special attention and keep this fixed in your mind. Every day when you wake up, you're going to remember you love yourself and everybody loves you. Remember again and believe that you love yourself and everybody loves you.

From now on, all your organs, especially your heart, your lungs, your liver, your stomach, your blood circulation, your kidneys and all your organs will do their respective work in a most harmonious and perfect way—and keep your body healthy and working in perfect harmony. All this is going to contribute to give you the most pleasant thoughts, a good mood, and a tremendous feeling of desire to live.

Beauty, love, peace and abundance from now on will be part of your life. And the essence of good will and the divine order will rule your whole life with happiness. This prayer is for you."
—Excerpt from the "Guided Imagery Sleep Healing" tape made for Cele by Dr. Harold Craselneck.

Hypnosis and guided imagery were next on our list. The two techniques share many similarities. The primary difference between the two is the level of intervention. While visualization, or guided imagery, creates a picture of what a hypnotherapist may want the client to consider or review, hypnosis suggests an intervention for the client, something both the therapist and client would like to change. Fine-tuning the mind and the thought patterns of another requires great skill and patience.

A psychologist, Dr. Harold Craselneck, in Dallas, was well-known for his abilities with hypnosis and guided imagery. He also happened to have a connection to our family through marriage—he was a relative of my former husband's.

I called and made the appointment. Mother was all for it as she had much confidence in the idea. I drove my mother to his office and sat in on her session. As Dr. Craselneck spoke to Mother in a soothing, clear, soft-spoken voice, I, too, was transfixed in my chair. Nothing unusual seemed to be going on. He was speaking directly to Mother in a normal tone. No one would have realized he was using hypnosis, which is a subtle art. His words made Mother feel that she was the most important person in the world—which was true during the session. He had a gift.

Dr. Craselneck gave Mother powerful suggestions to overcome the cancer. His philosophy and suggestions made a dovetail fit with my reality. When the one-hour session was over, Mother didn't think anything unusual had happened. She told us that she had felt awake and alert throughout the entire hour. The doctor looked confident. I was certain he had encountered this reaction many times with other patients. Still, she felt she hadn't been hypnotized. This worried me. I wanted to make sure Mother had confidence in what we were doing. I needed to confirm that she believed in everything that we undertook to help her get well. If she thought she was not actually hypnotized, then she would not believe that her session would be helpful.

We were assembling our forces to contain and defeat the cancer. There could be no chinks in the armor we were fashioning for her. There was no room for weakness. Each treatment was a fragment we were adding to our collage from which we could assemble a holistic picture of a cure.

Cluck Like a Chicken

Many people believe hypnosis is a form of mind control. Not so. Under hypnosis you may be entirely aware of what is happening at all times. You may also become so relaxed that you fall into a deeper trance that feels like sleep. You might even fall asleep.

Whatever level of trance you're in, you become more susceptible or responsive to suggestion. No one can make you do something you don't want to do—a misrepresentation that comes from entertainment, or stage hypnosis. Most of us have seen, for example, a variation of the hypnotist inducing his stage volunteers into a trance where they'd cluck like chickens in front of an amused but mystified audience. In truth, you are in control at all times and can stop the trance state whenever you choose—including those willing and clucking stage participants (who probably just needed an outlet for their exhibitionistic tendencies). Naturally, if you want positive and life-affirming hypnotic suggestions to take, you must allow them to happen. You must make positive thinking a moment-to-moment habit, like breathing.

My personal experience with hypnosis and guided imagery has been positive and productive. When I started medical school, I was extremely apprehensive about my new and difficult undertaking. I was scared I'd bitten off much more than I could chew. Also, I didn't feel prepared. Most of my classmates had taken four full years in pre-med whereas I had not. All I had taken were the prerequisites—biology, chemistry, organic chemistry and physics—which were required for admission into medical school. When I returned to college to take these prerequisite courses, I soon found out that they were merely "jump through the hoop" courses and of little help with the medical school curriculum.

Most of the time during my first year of medical school, I was stressed on different levels. I lived at home and commuted to classes daily.

The pressure and competitive pace at school were creating a barrier of tension between me and what I was studying. I had great difficulty in remembering what I had just studied. On top of that, I always felt behind in my studies and thought it was just me. I didn't realize at the time that most of the med students were feeling just as keenly unprepared. Being a proactive person, I knew I had to get on the right track with my studies—and sooner was better than later. We are all creatures of habit. I had stopped wetting the bed as a child after reaffirming my goal in the mirror—a form of self-hypnosis. Now, as a grown woman, it was no surprise that I returned to what had worked in the past.

I began seeing Dr. Richard Citrin, a psychologist at the Texas Christian University Counseling Center, who used hypnosis and guided imagery in his practice. I felt, and he agreed, that if I could relax and take that edge off just a little, I could learn and remember more easily. I was so focused on what I didn't know that learning anything new seemed almost impossible. During our sessions, Dr. Citrin used hypnosis to help me feel more relaxed and calm when I studied. He also made a special audiotape for me that contained guided imagery and positive suggestions. I would listen to the tape before studying and especially before taking my anatomy exams. Through hypnosis, he loosened the knot in my head that had been keeping me from absorbing the material. My sessions with Dr. Citrin, in combination with listening to my trusty tape, made the difference. Relaxed and focused, I was able to learn. We continued our professional relationship throughout my medical school education. I saw him often during my first year of school and needed his help less after that—a testament to his good work. Mimi had been on to the benefits of hypnosis when she was sick. Now, years later, I was using hypnosis to make the grade.

The Circle Is Complete

Dr. Craselneck had also recorded a guided imagery audiotape for Mother. To reinforce the positive messages, she could listen to it anytime—just as I had listened to my relaxation tapes in medical school. He gave Mother suggestions to see herself well and that she would handle the chemotherapy without becoming sick. He told her that each chemotherapy treatment and each radiation treatment were sending powerful agents to rid her body of the cancer. The tape was so helpful that Mother would get it out whenever she was feeling down about her illness, or anytime she needed some extra help during the course of her treatments. Words can heal, too.

Dr. Craselneck's office was in Dallas, an hour's drive from Fort Worth. To take Mother for her appointments, I had to take a day off from work. I loved what Dr. Craselneck was doing, but felt we needed someone closer to home. I called Dr. Citrin, my old friend from medical school. He gave me a highly recommended referral, a psychologist in Fort Worth who also employed guided imagery in his practice. Since this psychologist was local, Mother had the option of seeing him more frequently, or as often as necessary. When she felt well enough, she would drive herself and Daddy was there to take her whenever she didn't feel up to it. The new hypnotherapist helped Mother specifically with visualization. If you can see it, you can reach it. Using guided imagery, he taught her to attack the tumor by visualizing her white cells gobbling up the cancer. Mother played ball and did her part. She told him that she was visualizing thousands of strong white cells attacking the cancer. I was elated. Mother's troops were storming the dark castle. I could visualize victory. I could almost smell it.

Mother spent many hours each day visualizing her white cells destroying the cancer. During one office visit, after he'd hypnotized Mother, the doctor astutely questioned her again about how many white cells were attacking the cancer. While her conscious self visualized thousands of them, her subconscious mind saw only one. You can't fool yourself. It's a universal law. It seemed Mother could only muster one small, lonely, white blood cell to fight the great big cancer. Perhaps that was how Mother saw herself—one small, weak person fighting a giant enemy. That would not do! The word does become the flesh, your reality. Remember David and Goliath?

Mother's one white cell army needed reinforcements. Her deep-seated thoughts and feelings needed to be corrected immediately. Through hypnosis, the psychologist fortified her strength on both levels of awareness as he reconciled her conscious self with her subconscious through a series of positive suggestions. He also made sure that her unconscious brain, where so many of our autonomic bodily decisions are made, was sending thousands of white cells to attack the invading tumor. Thank goodness the doctor uncovered Cele's lopsided thought pattern early enough in her treatments to help her kill off the cancer—in her mind now and in her body later.

Chapter 16

By the Book: A Place for Nutrition

"It is difficult to get a man to understand something when his salary depends upon his not understanding it."
—Upton Sinclair

The medical field itself is a battleground, a minefield of conflicting opinions about nearly everything, and certain incomprehensible confusion for the uninformed. Is cancer caused by a virus? By bacteria? The fundamental answer and, consequently, the fundamental treatment depends upon whom you're asking. On a tastier note, for example, while one study indicated sugar inhibits the effectiveness of the immune system, another said cancer patients under treatment shouldn't rule out sweets to keep their weight up. In the fight against cancer, it seems there is sabotage at nearly every turn—often by the very agencies entrusted to treating the disease.

Informed and calculated decisions must be made if you're going to have a fighting chance against cancer. If you must take someone's word regarding a matter of life or death, be absolutely certain that your source is impeccable. Better yet, my life experience has taught me there is no substitute for finding out things firsthand. Or as Dr. C. Everett Koop, the former U.S. Surgeon General, put it: "The best prescription is knowledge." Getting in the trenches of the medical world and doing my own research had been essential in helping me locate the right healing situation for my daughter. I couldn't have saved Michelle any other way. Although I hadn't seen the value in it at the time, those doctors who had given up on my daughter did me a big favor. Their inept and regrettable behavior motivated me to push forward on my own to the solve the problem—something I would never have thought of doing on my own. I thought doctors knew it all. Sometimes our teachers in life are disguised as problems. Knowing all this, I was ahead of the game when it came to Mother's cancer. I wouldn't leave her shot at success in the hands of the partially informed.

When it comes to the importance of good nutrition while fighting cancer, there's no argument, although what is considered "good" often opens up a can of worms. Well-nourished patients can maintain their strength and stamina, better manage the side effects of chemotherapy and radiation, have fewer infections, and recover more quickly between treatments. A balanced diet also provides energy with enough calories to prevent weight loss, allowing stored protein to be used for building and repairing tissue, supporting the immune system and keeping the blood supply strong. A body not receiving enough calories will use the available stored protein for energy and not for repair, leaving itself without the critical mechanism for rebuilding normal body tissue and thus become more susceptible to disease.

When you're suffering severe nausea, constant vomiting, and appetite loss from chemotherapy and radiation, your body needs nutrients more than ever. I have a book called *Nutritional Influences on Illness* by Melvyn Werbach, MD. Divided into sections by diseases, this book contains hundreds of references from published medical literature concerning the importance of proper nutrition in fighting illness. I searched through the cancer section and wrote down every nutritional supplement that had ever been documented as helpful in fighting any kind of cancer. I added them to the regimen Mother had begun after our stealthy trip to the health food store.

To keep as up to date as possible on any medical break-throughs, I subscribed to *Clinical Pearls News,* a monthly "clipping service" newsletter, for doctors and laypeople, that summarizes hundreds of articles in nutrition and complementary medicine, similar in content to Werbach's book. Then, if I needed a copy of the entire article, I would write for it or go to the library and look up the source. In one day, I pored over several years of data from *Clinical Pearls,* looking for anything that had helped beat any kind of cancer. Again, I found a few more supplements for Mother's regimen. I knew that every positive fragment was really another solid brick on that yellow brick road toward Cele's picture of health (see Part Two of this book for information on supplements).

After a long and exhausting day of researching nutritional supplements, I made a beeline for my parents' house. When I arrived with yet a new list of supplements, Mother protested.

"It seems that all I do is take vitamins and minerals all day long. I don't think that I can put another one in my mouth!" she said.

Daddy was in the room. He shrugged and smiled. The ball was back in my court.

"Of course you can," I said calmly.

I explained why these additional supplements were needed and discussed the information I had found. I wanted Mother to know why she was doing everything she was doing. She wasn't going to get well by just going along. Each time she swallowed a vitamin or mineral I wanted her to think about how they were helping her get well. She needed to visualize nutritional supplements as part of her healing process.

Mother finally agreed. I left her and Daddy that evening feeling we had accomplished something significant toward saving her life.

During the next few days, I continued scouring the medical literature for anything that would help Cele. I became excited when I came across a medical article that said many people with cancer have high levels of calcium and low levels of magnesium. I poked further. Chocolate is a source of magnesium. A craving for chocolate could also be a sign of depression. I found several articles substantiating the magnesium connection. This was a definite call to action. I immediately began giving Mother magnesium injections twice a week. Since these injections require a 1½ inch needle to adequately penetrate the fat to underlying muscle mass, these shots can hurt. I did my best to give them as painlessly as possible. But Mother never complained. She would simply look at the needle and say: "Okay."

I thought back to the time when my grandmother needed someone to give her pain medication injections. I didn't have the stomach for it when Mimi needed me. Now, 18 years later, I was giving Mother injections. Mimi would have been proud of her formerly squeamish granddaughter who was now a doctor. I hoped my dear grandmother was watching how her strength had become my strength, and how our drama was playing out.

Mother needed vitamins and minerals. The only way to verify that she was absorbing the full benefit of her supplements was to administer them intravenously, bypassing her digestive system. We couldn't rely on her intestinal tract to do the job because you can never be sure they are absorbing efficiently. I wanted to be sure all the supplements were fed directly into her system where they would make it into the cells that needed them most. I think she disliked this treatment the most—well, probably not as much as chemotherapy. Mother is impatient and doesn't like to just sit. She likes to be up and about. To receive her supplements through the IVs, she had to sit quietly in the doctor's office for an hour, sometimes two, twice each week. To pass the time while the precious vitamins and minerals dripped into her vein, she read health-related magazines. One thing was for sure. Mother was extremely glad to get moving after each intravenous feeding at the IV station. She'd tell me so as we were leaving the doctor's office.

As much time, albeit passive, that I had spent with Mimi during her terminal bout with cancer, it was now abundantly clear that the memory of that episode was helping me in a strategic way with Cele. I wasn't that same young, naïve mother who had nearly fallen apart in the presence of this frightening and formidable disease. I was grateful that I had not merely grown older, but that I had developed into a woman of action who could make a difference. We don't always get the opportunity to make good on something we regret. What I was unable to do for Mimi, I could now do for Mother with more determination and tenacity than even I knew I possessed.

Barking Up the Right Tree

Mother took her medicine dutifully, as if her life depended on it. She promised to read the books I gave her and she did, including my dog-eared copy of *The Power of Positive Thinking* by *Norman Vincent Peale*—the very same copy that had helped me stop wetting the bed as a budding teenager. Mother surprised me one day. She was ill but still had plenty of spunk. From the stack of books I'd given her, she found an article on her own about a tea called pau d'arco, also known by the name of "taheebo," that offered a benefit in fighting cancer.

Pau d'arco tea, which had a distinct bitter bite to it, was made from the purple inner bark of the pau d'arco tree that grew predominately in Brazil and Argentina, and other tropical regions. The Incas referred to pau d'arco as "The Divine Tree" since it promoted health and was used for a variety of medicinal purposes, including cleansing the blood and as nutritional support for the immune system. Since pau d'arco was introduced in the United States in 1980, there had been strong evidence to support that the herb had strong antiviral, antifungal, and antibacterial properties. Mother began drinking pau d'arco tea every day. I knew that with each sip she was visualizing herself getting better and better. Cele from Fort Worth had reached out for help and the ancient Incas had answered from across the centuries with: "Time for tea."

Yes, I thought, Mother was really getting into this "healing thing" now.

Chapter 17

If It Can't Hurt—Or
Even If It Can

> *"I know God will not give me anything I can't handle. I just wish He didn't trust me so much."* —Mother Theresa

We weren't afraid to try anything in medicine if it might help and wouldn't hurt. I was committed to leaving no stone unturned. Anything I read or heard about that held out options for eliminating cancer became a candidate for Mother's regimen. Although I preferred that all of Mother's treatments would be completely safe and without concern of doing damage, there were two treatments that could do a great deal of damage—in fact, you could bet on it.

As I mentioned earlier, traditional Western medicine gives us three choices in treating cancer: surgery, radiation, and chemotherapy, graphically and accurately referred to as "slash, burn, and poison." Slash had been eliminated for Cele. No doctor was willing to perform surgery on my mother's tumor. It was too risky as it might cut into her aorta and she could bleed to death. Burn or poison alone was considered, at best, palliative. Radiation or chemotherapy might slow down the rate of the tumor's growth for a while but not eliminate the cancer.

Combining radiation with chemotherapy was the protocol offered by my friends and colleagues, Drs. Jordan and Friess. Although a great deal of damage could and would be done using this treatment, I wasn't going to ignore anything that might increase Cele's chances for life. Radiation could burn and damage my mother's lungs, and it did. Radiation can and did cause osteoporosis (a disease in which the bones become extremely porous and are subject to fracture), in the vertebrae in her back. Chemotherapy can and did damage Mother's white blood cells—the very same cells needed by the body's immune system to help fight cancer and other diseases. Chemotherapy also usually caused hair and weight loss, nausea, and vomiting. The cumulative effects of radiation and chemotherapy could debilitate a person to the point of death. Mother understood the consequences of burn and poison. She knew these therapies would be tough, especially the initial side effects of chemotherapy. Cele had watched Mimi go through it and she had many friends who had been treated for cancer as well. She was prepared to deal with it.

Someone with "good" intentions had suggested that Mother put ice on her head during the chemotherapy. Presumably the cold would prevent the chemotherapy from causing her hair to fall out. When Mother asked Dr. Friess about the ice during an office visit, he got visibly concerned. "Absolutely not!" he said. "Definitely, don't put ice on your head. The ice actually helps defeat our purpose by closing the blood vessels in your head, preventing the chemotherapy from reaching those areas." It's a good thing Mother asked.

Mimi didn't lose her hair during chemotherapy. She hadn't used ice on her head, or anything else to prevent hair loss. The chemotherapy didn't save her, either. In my constant quest to find meaning in everything, I suspected that there was a correlation between losing hair and the effectiveness of the chemotherapy. I told Mother, "If you lose your hair, it means the chemotherapy is working."

Although Mother hated just the thought of becoming bald, she could now see it in a new light—tangible evidence that the treatment was working. Each hair that would fall from her loving head would reinforce her visualization that yet another cancer cell had bitten the dust. There's nothing like having proof that something is working to keep you going.

Soon after the chemotherapy started, Mother's hair began falling out. "Hallelujah. Hallelujah," I said to Mother. "It's working. It's working." Cele was less than enthusiastic. She nodded and gave me her cute smile. Her head looked pretty awful with clumps of hair and stray strands sprinkled among the bald spots. Mother got up and walked over to a mirror in the living room. She looked at her reflection for a few minutes. I could tell she had made a decision. It was time for fake gold locks. She took a pair of scissors and made short work of what the chemotherapy had started. A friend lent Cele a few turbans to wear until she found a wig. Mother didn't complain and faced her baldness in her usual matter-of-fact manner. I'm sure our talk about hair loss being a confirmation that the chemotherapy was working helped put things in perspective for her, and for me.

The day came when she went out to buy a wig. Although Mother's hair had been naturally gray for many years, she colored it blonde. Mother took it upon herself to handle this job on her own. She found a woman who specialized in fitting wigs for cancer patients going through chemotherapy. After a rigorous round of tryouts, she bought a silky blonde wig with a natural-looking sheen that felt just right. Mother showed me her wig after she'd purchased it. She was pleased with her decision, which was good for morale all around. Cele wore her wig through the entire treatment phase and during the time it took for her hair to grow out again—which she proudly decided to leave a lovely gray.

I felt angry and resented that Mother had to be subjected to the devastation of radiation and chemotherapy, which would undoubtedly cause major body damage. I did my best not to show my negative feelings to Mother. I had to keep the larger picture in mind—always. With luck, the damage wouldn't be irreparable. Then, there was yet another "what if" issue. What if we didn't do poison and burn and she died? How would I feel? There's nothing harder than being a doctor—knowing all you do about medicine—and yet not being able to save someone you love. Here I was a doctor and a daughter feeling a double dose of frustration in trying to save Mother. We had gone to the M.D. Anderson Cancer Center for a cure and returned with Mother's cancer still growing strong. Although it turned out that the center wasn't helpful, I was afraid I would regret not making the pilgrimage to Houston. How do you know where the answers are if you don't look everywhere for them? The answer, as always, is in the last place you look.

As I watched Mother become sick, weak, and lose her hair, I admired her more and more with each passing day. Although her physical self was falling apart, she was still holding together emotionally and spiritually. I wondered if it would last. I wondered if I would be able to go through such torture if it ever became necessary.

While Mother was going through the rough grind of cancer therapy, I kept reinforcing that Dr. Friess's treatment was having great success with other patients. Again, it was essential she believe that everything we were doing would be successful. It had to be her mantra, every moment, every hour, every day, every week, and every month—until she was healed. As each ray of radiation penetrated her body and each drop of chemotherapy dripped into her system, she had to visualize that burn and poison were eradicating the cancer.

Cele took pride in her appearance. She kept herself trim and never allowed herself to gain more than five pounds above her ideal weight—an especially formidable feat for someone who loves sweets. Keeping her weight down wasn't going to be a problem now. Feeling nauseated and vomiting frequently from chemotherapy, eating was not at the top of her list of enjoyable activities. It was essential that she *not* lose too much weight. People with cancer can become cachectic, a word meaning wasting away—not a good sign. Mother's job was to keep her weight *on*. I knew her twice-weekly vitamin and mineral IVs, which she liked the least, were preventing her from wasting away.

Choosing Priorities

As I previously mentioned, I had started my private practice a few months before my mother was diagnosed with lung cancer. As a new doctor, I wasn't initially packed with patients but things changed quickly. An article that ran in my local newspaper about my non-drug approach to Attention Deficit Hyperactivity Disorder (ADHD) brought in a steady stream of new patients. My practice was booming and I was pleased. Still, there was a dilemma. Though my current priority was one patient, my mother, at the same time, I had an obligation to care for the people coming to me to get well.

One day, a few hours after her chemotherapy treatment, Mother became intensely ill and had to be rushed to the emergency room at the Osteopathic Medical Center of Texas where I was on staff. Mother collapsed upon arrival. Daddy called me. I was in the middle of an office visit with one of my young patients. I explained the situation to the patient's family, suggested they reschedule, and rushed off to the emergency room. I never heard from that family again and I can't blame them. Leaving my patients during an office visit wasn't going to help me develop and maintain a successful medical practice. Well, I thought, I didn't leave anyone hanging on for dear life—at least, not yet.

From the day I opened my practice, my patients received my full attention but the emergency situations with Mother forced me to pull back. My reason for becoming a doctor was to help my family—job number one. What I'd learned as a mother, wife, and daughter contributed to making me the kind of doctor I had sought out when my family needed help. What I learned in helping Mother introduced me to new possibilities, which translated into more options and hope for many of my patients. I'm a better person and physician for having faith in my values and duty as a loving daughter. I have compassion for my patients. I've walked in their shoes. When Mother needed me, I had to go with my gut reaction.

I realized I may have put off some of my patients with my "see you later I have an emergency" behavior. It's the price of doing the right thing. My priority was my mother. There was no doubt. All of my stamina was devoted to her. It consumed my every waking moment. At night, my dreams of seeing Mother healthy were so real I could nearly touch Cele's healed body.

Although I couldn't yet prove it, I knew in the long run that my dedication to Mother would pay off for her, me, and my more patient patients.

Chapter 18

Future Perfect

"Cele and her daughter, Mary Ann, are remarkably alike. Both are hard-headed and very determined!" —Dr. Richard Citrin

Just as her mother Mimi had done, my mother endured chemotherapy and radiation without complaining. In the midst of getting poisoned and burned, she did her best to attend every party or luncheon with her friends. Keeping mentally and physically alert helped distract her from what she was going through. It would have been easy to lie in bed and feel sorry for herself. But self-pity wasn't my mother's style. She was up, dressed, wig in place, and active every day that she could manage it.

Then, there were days when she was too sick and too weak to get out of bed. Those were the days I dreaded and feared most—seeing Mother's life being squeezed out of her in front of my eyes. The clock was ticking. My ability to hold the reality of success together could fracture at any moment. I couldn't let my guard down for a second—doubt can corrupt and take over before you know it. On her really bad days, I would take a deep breath and visualize Mother waltzing through my front door with an announcement: "I'm cancer free!" Mother would be a survivor, not a statistic. Bold words for an absolute reality, and necessary when you're going for the impossible.

In the middle of one particular night, Mother awoke and got

out of bed to go to the bathroom. Daddy, hearing the unmistakable thud of flesh and bone hitting the floor, knew Cele had fallen. Daddy rushed into the bathroom and found his wife unconscious. She was so weak that she had collapsed. Daddy kept his wits about him and dialed 911 for an ambulance, then me. Since I live a couple of blocks away, I rushed out in a robe and was there before the paramedics. Lying on the bathroom floor in a half-dazed state, Mother was sufficiently alert enough to know what had happened to her. She thought she was O.K. When the paramedics arrived on the scene with their life-saving equipment and saw a bald 75-year-old woman sprawled like a rag doll on the bathroom floor, they asked me if she was DNR—"Do Not Resuscitate." The term is used when someone has a terminal illness and doesn't want any extraordinary medical treatment or extravagant lifesaving measures taken to revive them.

I told the paramedics, "No way! She's no DNR!"

I had seen many patients at the Osteopathic Medical Center of Texas where I did my internship who were candidates for DNR. These terminally ill patients were dying and no one was standing in their way. I'm no moralist when it comes to private acts of conscience. When a person has no hope of survival, or of living a productive life, and they don't want to be placed on a respirator (or any other life-sustaining equipment) to stay alive, DNR is an option. Yes, my mother was sick and weak from cancer and the invasive therapies. But she was not DNR! As I stepped back for a moment, I had to admit she did look pretty pitiful on the bathroom floor and I could see why the paramedics had asked the question.

Philosophically Speaking

Is there a point in time when living is too costly? Mimi suffered unspeakable pain and was able to defy it. She was the iron lady. Someone else might not have the same pain threshold. Death for them would be a blessing. The right to live has to be balanced with the right to die. Only those who have suffered the agony of crippling pain understand the lure and peace offered by death. Anyone else can only empathize and imagine the magnitude of such intolerable pain and the decision to put an end to one's life. Our desires and needs may have nothing at all in common with those of the patient. The red herring in all the deceptive arguments for protecting those who want out is society's right to infringe upon the individual's rights to protect him from himself.

Over the years, Dr. Jack Kevorkian, a name in the public eye, has been trying to make his case in the court system by participating in physician-assisted suicide. He has brought a great deal of national attention on dying and severely ill people who have had enough. My parents agree with Dr. Kevorkian to this extent. A person who is terminally ill, in severe pain that cannot be relieved, or is so mentally or physically incapacitated that living any kind of productive life is impossible, should have the right to end his own life. Neither of my parents wishes to remain on life support if such a tragedy should befall them. They made their choice to let nature take its course if and when they should become mentally incompetent. This is family business. No federal government agencies need apply here.

Had the paramedics in the middle of the night observed something I hadn't, or rather refused to see? Was my bald-headed mother dying right in front of my eyes? Was I in denial again and wouldn't acknowledge it? Was she going through the misery of chemotherapy and radiation for me? Was I giving out that unsaid message that I couldn't let go? Was I doing the very same thing to my mother that I had done to my grandmother? Was I doing the thing that I had promised myself I would never do ever again to someone I love? The hastiness of never was on the vulture's wing and I felt its presence circling and circling with endless patience.

My mother and I are so close that I don't believe I will ever know the answer to these questions. Maybe there is no single truth in such situations, only an event with infinite points of view and interpretations. Even if it were my determination to keep her alive that was driving her to endure the pain, I knew she would never consciously recognize it. She wanted to live, of course, for me, and for herself as well. After all, it was she who took the initiative and selected a visualization process that focused on the future, something she wanted to be alive to see.

A Member of the Wedding

When Mother and I were discussing what she should visualize, she came up with a theme that I thought was a great idea. She decided to visualize her grandchildren's weddings. Mother has four grandchildren: three girls and one boy. Twins Lauren and Tracy are my brother's children, and Michelle is my daughter. My son, Randy, is the only boy and the youngest grandchild. He's two years younger than the girls who were all about 20 years old at the time.

Mother's goal in her visualization was to be at their weddings and walk down the aisle for each grandchild. Since her granddaughters were older and female, she expected them to get married before Randy. Mother was pushing the envelope. She visualized herself at Randy's wedding. He was 18 years old at the time and the men in our family were not noted for marrying young. Mother felt pretty sure that his wedding was, at least, ten years off. Every day she visualized herself participating in Randy's wedding. She saw herself shopping for her "Grandmother of the Groom" dress. She saw herself walking down the aisle as a member of the wedding. She saw it all in her mind's eye because she wanted to be there for real. If she could be alive ten years from now to be at Randy's wedding, it meant cancer had not killed her. It seemed like a good plan to me—the best as it would turn out—and it fit perfectly into my reality. My mother knew how to pick her visualization as I would come to learn. One day, we would all catch up with her vision of future events; one day she would walk down the aisle with Randy at Michelle's wedding. One day at a time.

In my medical practice, I work with chronic health problems in adults and children—especially those who have been diagnosed with Attention Deficit Hyperactivity Disorder (ADHD). In most cases, my young patients come to me already on medications such as Ritalin. Instead of prescribing drugs, I prefer to fix the problem by exposing the underlying cause of behavioral attention, or learning problems. In my first book, *No More Ritalin, Treating ADHD Without Drugs*, I go into my protocol in depth. Since I don't go for the "quick fix," it may take a while to rule out the possible causes and get to the bottom of the problem. If I'm working closely with a family over a period of time, it's not unusual for us to become friends.

One day, the young mother of one of my child patients called and made an appointment to see me. When she walked into my office, she was ashen and visibly distraught. Although she was not my patient, she felt comfortable enough with me to confide that her doctor had found a lump in her breast. Her doctors were concerned that it was cancerous. A biopsy had been scheduled for the following week—an eternity for the patient, an eternity that I knew so well. She asked if I could suggest anything to help her get through the awful waiting game. She couldn't bear the thought of dying and leaving her two young boys without a mother. I suggested she stop thinking of the worst, which is a tendency that's learned and can be unlearned and get into the habit of seeing and focusing on the positive. I told this young mom to do what my mother had done.

"Anytime you get down and depressed," I said, "visualize yourself many years into the future at the wedding of your two boys."

My advice was brief, yet potent. She thanked me and left looking better. I hoped my suggestion would help her through her long week of waiting to hear what kind of hand she'd been dealt. I knew the stress of the situation firsthand. I called her a couple of days later to see how she was holding up.

Her voice sounded much stronger than when I had seen her in my office. She said, "I'm doing very well. Whenever I feel down, I just picture myself at one of the weddings and I feel O.K. again. By the way, do you think it's O.K. to wear blue as mother of the groom?"

We laughed. She was doing a good job of visualizing. Getting into the details such as what color dress she would be wearing was an important factor for a successful visualization. The more details she could conjure up, the more real the visualization would be. That's how we build our own reality. Following Mother's visualization scheme definitely helped this young mom survive the week with less stress.

After her biopsy, she called me and reported her tale. Her doctors had told her that even before they cut into her breast, they had expected the worst—what a nightmare. Whatever happened to let's hope for the best? On her mammogram, the affected region showed possible signs of cancer. After they had cut into her breast and found the tumor, they were sure it was cancer. The growth felt like cancer and looked like cancer. When they got the tumor to the lab and looked at its cells under a microscope, they found the lump was benign. Of course, she was thrilled beyond words. A reprieve from the Great Creator.

"Do you think," she said to me over the phone, "that visualizing for just one week could have actually turned that lump from being cancerous into one that's benign?"

I had no answer for her. Certainly, anything was possible. I did know that being a mother is a powerful thing. A mother with a vision can change reality and alter destiny. If you think you can, you can. If you think you can't, you can't. Yes, why couldn't the power of visualization transmute a cancer into a harmless growth? It sounds impossible. Still, the impossible just takes getting used to by more and more people until it's a fact, until it's the four-minute mile.

Seeing herself at the wedding of her boys was precisely the prescription this mother had needed. I thanked Cele for giving me the concept for the visualization. Mother was very pleased that she was able to be so helpful. Good thoughts and ideas need to be passed along generously and in good spirit. You get what you give. WARNING: knowing this will change your life.

Chapter 19

ꕀ

Serving Up Hope
du Jour

"My motivation was 50-25-25. Fifty percent for the survivors of cancer and those in the cancer community who helped me survive. Twenty-five percent was for me and my teammates. And twenty-five percent was for those people who didn't believe in me." —Champion cyclist, Lance Armstrong, two-time winner of the three-week, 2,287-mile Tour de France for 1999 and 2000

Mother was a trouper. She had an indomitable spirit. She was human, too. At a low point in her treatment, my mother called me one afternoon at my office and whispered that she was depressed—which must have been difficult for this feisty lady to admit. On the one hand, I didn't want to hear it. On the other hand, who could fault her for feeling down. I wouldn't have known she was feeling down if she hadn't told me. Cele loved to socialize. Sure, she was often sick from the chemotherapy and the treatments had laid waste to her appetite, energy, and strength. Still, she rarely appeared low and was amazingly even-keeled most of the time. She "never" missed a party, a card game, or a night out with her friends. Now, suddenly, it seemed she could think of only one thing.

"Mary Ann," she said, her voice sounding especially frail over the phone, "I've been thinking. It seems to me that every person I've ever read or heard about who had lung cancer has died."

Her words fell like bricks on my head. Hey, I thought, those bricks were for the road, not for clobbering us into depression.

Cele was waiting for my reply. I was stuck. Mother was developing a negative visualization and that wasn't the healthy choice. Such thoughts could easily blow our whole effort, our whole campaign to save her.

At times you can hold the whole world together with seemingly no effort at all; at other times, your world starts to unravel and you can't remember how you had kept it together in the first place. Remaining positive in the face of adversity is demanding—second by second you keep your world from dissolving. No one said it would be easy. Mother was undergoing the ravages of chemotherapy and radiation, feeling nauseous, vomiting, losing weight and her hair. Who wouldn't feel demoralized? Still, I felt it was essential that she not be depressed. Her immune system would weaken with the slightest chink in her protective armor.

This was a critical juncture on Cele's path to wellness. Depression can derail the best of us. Feeling a bit down about this or that is one thing. A healthy person can bounce back. A cancer patient is another matter. The forces working against the body from the cancer and invasive treatments are enormously destructive. Bouncing back into life for the cancer patient is an incredible act of will. A weak, unsuspecting moment is all that depression requires. No one is above it. You must fight to live. This isn't my idea. Nature demands it. Would Mother turn toward life, or not? Depression can dim the light of hope until there's only an ember of gloom, and then only the darkness. Her job was to remain strong. We both knew it but she needed to hear it again and again from me. She needed to feel her power over her cancer. She needed to genuinely believe and have faith that the combination of treatments we had carefully orchestrated would eventually eradicate every single cancer cell from her body. We had to believe. It was a matter of life.

Mother was still waiting patiently on the phone, waiting for me to say something. I had time to collect my thoughts.

"Mother. I'm with you. I understand. It's only human to get a bit depressed over what you've been going through. I know you're feeling bad right now and I know it will pass. Isn't that what you taught me about dealing with problems? The main thing here is for you not to worry. You need that strength to keep you alive."

I know my mother. When you love someone, you pick up the slightest hesitation or intonation. You know when things are in dissonance. There is no question. Cele didn't sound too convinced with my reply, but perked up when I added: "I'll be over right after work." Until then, I reminded her that listening to the guided imagery tape Dr. Craselneck made for her was a good idea.

When I arrived at my parents' house that evening, they were sitting in their chairs in the bedroom. Mother saw I had my doctor's black bag in hand and gave me one of her cute smiles. She knew the drill. Magnesium was on the way. She got ready for the big needle. I'm sure she would have preferred eating her fill of chocolates for her mega-magnesium dose. I gave her the shot in the hip area. Although she didn't wince, I did on the inside. In my research I had already determined that cancer patients were deficient in magnesium. In addition, I had also discovered that magnesium had been shown to be one of the first minerals to leave the body under stress. Furthermore, case studies indicated that magnesium was beneficial in treating depression—the chocolate connection again. Anything that wouldn't hurt—well, maybe hurt some—and that would help, was on my list.

It's just as important to recognize our limits as it is our limitless horizon. Asking for help isn't easy and Mother needed more than I could provide alone. After mother's shot, I brought up the idea of her seeing Dr. Richard Citrin, the psychologist who had hypnotized me in medical school to help me with my studies. Mother would be able to talk to him about her concerns and fears in a context different from her daughter. She gave me a nod of agreement. Cele followed my doctor's orders. To give orders, you have to know how to take them as well. I told Mother I'd call the doctor the next day to make an appointment for her.

That evening, I left my mother feeling much better. We had gotten back on track. The physical act of getting her magnesium shot seemed to have taken the edge off. Mother promised to listen to her visualization tape that night and she made a point of telling me that she was looking forward to her session with Dr. Citrin.

Several days later, I spoke with Dr. Citrin over the phone. He told me his session with my mother had been very different.

"How so?" I asked.

"She didn't cry and feel sorry for herself," he said. "She didn't ask 'Why me?' She told me matter-of-factly that 'I just don't have a role model for dying so I just don't think I will die.'"

Dr. Citrin had never heard anyone say anything like that before. Her comments about a lack of a role model for death surprised him in the sense that folks her age usually have considered issues of death, or avoided looking at them. Although such a response may suggest a kind of naiveté about death, that wasn't the case with Cele. Mother's unique perspective on death would serve her well and play a pivotal role in her recovery. Years after Cele had beaten her lung cancer, her oncologist, Dr. Friess, would tell me how he continues to be amazed at her long-term remission. In response, I would tell him about Mother, who was under his treatment at the time, informing a psychologist that she can't die because "I don't have a role model for dying." Dr. Friess would nod his head knowingly and in affirmation, saying, "Mary Ann, that's the real reason she's alive." This exchange would not take place for many years and wouldn't have taken place at all if Cele hadn't had such a remarkable outlook on death.

I felt Dr. Citrin's assessment of Mother was right on. He filled me in on his observations—things I knew, yet were always great to hear from others. He felt Cele was a person who appeared to live gently in the world, which is a prime skill for handling longevity. Her steps were light. When she sat or stood up, she did so gracefully. Cele was comfortable with her body, although angry at its betrayal. Her emotions were well managed and realistic. She didn't hide from her feelings, honoring them and their place in her life. At the same time, she wouldn't give into them, or let them overwhelm her.

"She's just remarkably centered," he said. "Your mother is prepared to face her cancer head on."

This was spectacular news. I couldn't have been happier than to hear Dr. Citrin's conclusion. It meant that Mother had no intention of dying. It was April 1991, and it looked as if she was going to live past Mother's Day. Cele's depression didn't manifest itself during her session with Dr. Citrin. I suspect that the very act of seeing him helped her move into a better space.

Thinking positive sounds almost too easy, which it isn't. Take a moment and investigate what this really means. Try counting the number of positive and negative thoughts you have in just one day of your life. I think you'll be surprised, maybe shocked. I do know that you have to open up your heart to new ways of seeing the world, to new ways of healing yourself. I feel the heart needs to be seen in a wider context than the localized pumping organ. Feeling is intuitive and I was following my intuition to help save my mother. No amount of conceptualizing will ever put anyone in touch with their intuition, their innate ability to feel the truth. You must feel and believe in what you are doing for it to work. Mother was still in the running. Winning the race meant life.

We, as a family, never told my grandmother she had cancer, or that it would most likely kill her. We also never came out and told her how much we all loved her, how important she was to us, and how much we would miss her when she was gone. Although I know in my heart that Mimi was aware of our great love for her, we were afraid to express our sentiments since they would give away our secret fear and Mimi's fate—that she was dying. There was no treatment available that I knew about back then that was going to save Mimi. Knowing this, I don't feel our vow of silence about her cancer had been necessarily wrong. With the passage of time, I've come to realize that dear Mimi, despite our secret, undoubtedly knew the score all along.

Laughter: The Best Medicine

There was no way my mother was going to die without knowing how I felt right up front. I had come far. I was no longer that squeamish young housewife who couldn't let go of her grandmother. But I had to walk a fine line, a tightrope that could only be traversed by using tact and love for a balance pole. Therefore, it was important that I convey my love and feelings for Mother in a way that didn't imply she was going to die. While I wanted her to continue believing that she would survive, I also wanted her to know how I felt in case she didn't. I was definitely on the high wire and so was the rest of my family—we had no safety net.

Like Mimi, I suspect Mother knew all along how seriously ill she was. At one point, she gave me a ring, a gold band, she had made herself in a jewelry making class. I had a strong feeling that she was scared. She thought it was possible that she might not live. She wanted me to have the ring. Just like I did with Mimi's ring, I put the ring on my finger and have not taken it off since. I wear Mimi's ring on my left hand and Mother's on my right. With such strong energy between them, my life is guaranteed to be safe.

As a family, we had not been a particularly demonstrative one when it came to conveying emotions. We were definitely not of the touchy-feely persuasion. The love we felt for one another expressed itself through actions. We were always there for each other. You could bet the farm on it. We held each other in the highest regard and treated one another with respect. We didn't take one another for granted, the sure road to family squabbling. Nor did we yell at or abuse one another to make a point. It just wasn't necessary. The love and caring that we felt over the years had always been there—most often unsaid, yet never overlooked.

Timing is everything. I'll speak for the family. None of us had felt like celebrating a few months earlier. Mother's birthday came around soon after she had begun her chemotherapy and radiation. At that time, we were still in shock. Life felt out of sync. Trying to be jolly at her birthday would have been forcing the issue and our enthusiasm would have been artificial—and Cele would have felt it.

Now, with the passing weeks, we were doing something about Mother's cancer. The momentum to celebrate had been building within me. I felt a party coming on, a grand and unusual gathering to be specific—life was feeling in alignment. I was determined that this upcoming Mother's Day wasn't going to pass into the stratosphere with all of those words still unspoken, still unheard. I wanted to break free of tradition. I wanted my family to let their hair down—naturally, Mother was already ahead of the game in that area. I called my brother, Steve, in Houston. We agreed and planned a special Mother's Day weekend that included dinner at my house and brunch the next day.

When Mother was first diagnosed with lung cancer, I had given her a book by Norman Cousins called *Anatomy of An*

Illness that illustrated the lifesaving benefits to be gained through taking responsibility for one's own well-being. Cousins had miraculously cured himself of a rare and supposedly terminal blood disease with a remedy called laughter, which he proved was the best medicine of all. He watched comedy shows that made him laugh day in and day out. Laughter was good for the spirit, and that could only translate into helping the body's immune system. I knew laughter would be good for Mother, too, and it certainly wouldn't hurt. I still had hope that this cancer would become an-out-of-body experience for her. I had to be honest with myself. I couldn't be certain of what would happen. Just in case, I made sure that her family would make this the best and most memorable Mother's Day ever.

My mother is a great lady. I'm fortunate to have her as my mother. Cele personifies "Mother." She always made the world O.K. for me and my brother. I always wanted to return her gift. Now it was my turn to make the world right for her. As Mark Twain observed: "Kindness is the language which the deaf can hear and the blind can see."

Mother knew we were doing the dinner and the brunch and that the whole family would be there. She didn't know that we had planned entertainment or that I had made up a new recipe which I called Chicken Cecile. All the others—Steve, Gail, Lauren, Tracy, Michelle, Randy, Daddy, and I—wrote poems, ditties, and skits. We took lots of pictures and videos. As soon as we began singing our original songs, something magical happened. Inhibitions went out the window as the muse of delight entered. We were free to be as warm, loving, funny, and as silly as we wished. It was all the more miraculous as no one in our family can carry a tune. When I say we sang, the word sang should be in quotation marks. Most importantly, we were singing with feeling from the heart and laughing at our off-key solos and duets. Our chorus attempts fared better as voices homogenized into a semblance of harmony.

Mother had always been a good audience. When something hit her funny bone she would often start laughing uncontrollably and not be able to stop. It was quite a wonderful sight to see my poised Mother breaking up over our antics. As we cavorted and made merry, my father and mother sat next to each other while we—their children and grandchildren—surrounded them with smiles, singing, and an abundance of laughter. We were alive and making the most of each moment despite the dire circumstances. Mimi had taught me that lesson. I felt it was poetic that we should break the family mold and let Cele know directly how much we loved her on Mother's Day. The climate in my home on that special day in May was remarkably free and spontaneous. The uninvited guest called death was not missed. Whether this would be Cele's last Mother's Day was left unspoken. As for me, my hope was incurable.

Chapter 20

Killing Her Softly

"To win you have to risk loss." —Jean-Claude Killy

Mother's Day had been a tonic that Cele really needed. Soon after the festivities, she once again became very ill after a chemotherapy treatment. Mother might go down, but she was never out. Just when it looked as if she could take no more, she'd rise up to whatever was necessary. She was taking things one day at a time, taking one treatment at a time until the protocol would be over. Life had become a routine of treatments, feeling awful afterward, and hoping for the best to arrive very soon.

Mother was receiving radiation and chemotherapy concurrently. The radiation therapy was every day for three months. She completed her last radiation treatment on April 23, 1991. Less than one week after Mother's Day, Mother had another one of her chemotherapy treatments. Before each treatment, they'd give Mother a blood test. What can a droplet of blood reveal? A fascinating microscopic world that keeps us well, or not. Red and white blood cells, plasma, platelets, and fat particles to name a few. This time, Mother's white count was 1100 (normal: 3900-13,000), her platelets were 65 (normal: 140-400) and her hemoglobin and hematocrit were 9.8 and 28.1 (normal: 11-14 and 33-42). Her blood parameters were extremely low—not an omen of good news.

Dr. Jordan called Mother in for a conference. Mother saw Dr. Jordan regularly, but this time he wanted me there, too. I knew her blood count was low and that she had gone to the hospital for an X ray the week before. We didn't know the results yet and I feared the worst. I'm only human, too. I was afraid the cancer had spread or that he was going to stop the chemotherapy because it was making her sick and her white cell count was so low. Mother had only one more round of chemotherapy to go— one more lap to the finish line of her four-minute mile. Would her doctor let her complete the treatment with such low numbers in her blood? My head was already buzzing, trying to come up with plans of what we would do instead of chemotherapy.

Mother and I arrived at Dr. Jordan's office the next day. We didn't know what to expect. My knees felt wobbly. Mother looked around the waiting room as if she were seeing it for the first time. As usual, I acted as if nothing was wrong, always keeping a stiff upper lip and being positive. A nurse took us into an examination room. Mother sat on the exam table, I in a chair. We waited for the doctor. When Dr. Jordan came in he began talking in an upbeat yet serious tone.

He dived right in. "Remember," he said, "when we first met, I told you that chemotherapy is poison. What we hope to do with chemotherapy is to kill the cancer before we kill the patient."

My heart had already jumped into my throat. I said nothing.

He turned toward me, saying, "If we continue the chemotherapy on your mother, it will surely kill her." His words felt like bullets penetrating my less than bulletproof reality. Mother listened to the doctor and even though she nodded, I'm not certain she was really clear about what he meant in that moment. She was prepared to continue the chemotherapy no matter how bad she felt since she was sure it was helping her.

With the help of two new FDA-approved drugs that kept her white blood cell count up and quelled the vomiting and nausea, Cele had made it through the chemotherapy this far. Mother wanted to finish taking her poison. If she didn't, she might start thinking the chemotherapy hadn't worked after all—giving the cancer an edge. With only one full round of chemotherapy remaining, neither of us wanted to stop now that the light at the end of the tunnel was just up ahead. My head was spinning. I felt as if my reality were being unraveled right in front of me. I took a deep breath.

Dr. Jordan shifted our attention. "Besides, take a look at this," he said in a comfortable tone. He sure is one cool customer, I thought. Caring and detached was the right professional balance. Otherwise, you'd burn yourself out as an oncologist in no time at all.

He stood, picked up an X ray from his desk, and clipped it onto the view box mounted on the wall. He motioned for us to come up and take a look. Mother and I got up and scrutinized the picture. Something was definitely different. I remembered Mother's X ray when she'd been diagnosed with lung cancer four months earlier. I remembered how that great big, ominous mass had lodged itself right in the middle of her chest. The X ray Dr. Jordan was showing us now didn't have a tumor. At least, I couldn't see it.

"Is this my mother?" I asked, puzzled that my friend and colleague was showing us someone else's X ray for some purpose yet to be revealed.

Dr. Jordan looked me in the eye without acknowledging my question. In a blink, he shifted his attention to Cele. "As I said, if we continued the chemotherapy it will kill you. But, as you can now see for yourself, there's absolutely no reason to continue. The cancer is gone."

The cancer was gone.

We couldn't believe our ears or our eyes. Those were surely

among the four most beautiful words I had ever heard. "The cancer is gone!" My mother was going to live! We had done it. I hugged my mother. I was ready to dance. We hugged the doctor, too. Mother and I were smiling and crying at the same time.

Dr. Jordan brought us back to earth.

He cautioned us: "In oncology, there's really no such thing as a cure. It's all judged by the length of survival."

Sure, I thought, he was right. His summary did sound like a line out of an Alcoholics Anonymous meeting. Cure is all about time. In this instance, however, Mother had triumphed. This was a moment to savor, a moment to remember, and a moment to connect with the power of love and will. We left Dr. Jordan's office as two happy campers. When we got home and told Daddy, he cried. Although he had been pretty much stoic through the entire treatment phase, I knew Daddy was going through hell with Mother every day.

Afterward, Dr. Jordan sent mother for additional diagnostic tests over the next several days. Even though the X ray looked clear, the cancer could have migrated somewhere else. Cele had more tests—an MRI, a CT scan, plus a bone scan to make sure the cancer had been completely eradicated from her body. We waited anxiously for all the test results to come in. Fortunately, there was no need for concern. Anxiety melted into a deep sigh of relief. All three tests were conclusive: the tumor had been reduced to the most beautiful scar tissue imaginable. My mother was alive and cancer-free, words I had been "dying" to say out loud for the world to hear, for me and Mother to hear.

Battle Fatigue

At first, we began by celebrating with family members only. Just because the tumor was apparently gone did not mean it would not return. Mother eventually told some of her friends. Of course, everyone was exhilarated when they heard the news. But she was still so sick from the chemotherapy, none of them could yet grasp that she was really going to be okay, which, in fact, she wasn't.

What happened next took me completely by surprise. For every plus, there is a minus, which is the inexorable duality of all experience in our universe. In the midst of "victory," there was also a letdown. Mother had been investing all of her waning energy into survival. Her entire world had revolved around the cancer treatment, the protocols, and positive thinking. Now, her world had abruptly tuned into a new channel. Her doctor had given her the news we all wanted to hear. The cancer that was supposed to have killed her was gone. We were all elated.

When you put your entire being into a goal and then you're told that the effort is no longer necessary, there can be a tremendous emotional backlash—a letdown, a falling apart. It's not uncommon for a person to become ill after accomplishing an all-consuming event. When I was in medical school, I remember completing a set of final exams. I had worked hard and long on them. When they were over, I collapsed and came down with a respiratory infection. My experience was in no way unusual. Many other students experienced similar symptoms after completing an all-out intense task. Your body and mind get used to the steady pressure. Remove the pressure and you create a vacuum—with no place to go. You've got to prepare yourself for success.

Mother was no exception when it came to her post-success syndrome. When your body is under attack, bouncing back to health and living up to being disease free takes yet another leap of faith. Not that she had an alternative if she wanted to live. Still, after investing all of herself with time, energy, and focus into staying alive, she was now being told that she could stop

the therapies. For all those grueling months, she had been visualizing a future. Now, she could actually plan one. Good news
can be hard to take.

When Mother did let down, her body wasn't prepared. She
had been like a muscle, tightly flexed to fend off the disease.
Once the muscle relaxed, her emotional, mental, and physio-
logical strength turned to mush. After all, she had just been poisoned and burned. Cele had to recover from the assault and fear.
In most cases, there's no support system in place for handling
the peculiar aftereffects of beating cancer. Other than follow-up
CTs, MRIs, X rays and bone scans, the work of the oncologist is
done. I felt that since she had conquered the cancer, all was fine
now and we could all resume a normal life, forever grateful that
Mother was going to live. We see what we want to see and I was
exuberantly naïve.

It wasn't going to be quite as easy as I had pictured it. I was
sure we'd be home free, celebrating life each day forever, once
the cancer had been beaten. My reality felt whole, yet I knew it
needed some fine-tuning if we were to persevere. Mother led
the way. She lived through the cure. Killing the cancer was the
first step in the recovery process. It was time to move along toward step two. Since I wasn't sure there was going to be a second step, I didn't know what that next step should be, or what it
looked like. I certainly wasn't alone. With more and more people living after cancer treatment, I felt after-cancer care needed
to include recovery and support groups as a matter of course.
Knowing about this post-cancer letdown might have prepared
us for it. Instead, Mother and I had to land on our feet running
toward an answer.

Fallout from the Cure

Now that the challenge of killing the cancer had been overcome, we had to deal with other aftereffects of the physical kind. Mother's white blood cell count was still dangerously low. Since she no longer needed chemotherapy, her white cells could, if all went well, begin increasing on their own—this is the body healing itself. The radiation therapy had burned her lungs and left them permanently scarred, which manifested as a bad chronic cough compounded by breathing problems similar to asthma. Radiation had also caused Mother to develop osteoporosis and a compression fracture of the vertebra in her middle back that left her in constant pain.

Though we had won—Mother was free of cancer—she was not healthy. Had we taken one step forward and two steps back? Then again, at least we were still stepping.

Mother's back pain from the radiation was constant. She had few reserves left to put up yet another fight. She was tired, weak, and in constant misery. After struggling with all her might to live, she didn't want to end up living in agony—an awful price for cheating death. This situation scared me.

We got on the physician carousel and began seeing more doctors once again. I felt I had been living through a bad dream for three months, a fourth of a year, a lifetime. Now, I was waking up to a new nightmare, not the dream I had been visualizing. You must work harder, Mary Ann, I said to myself. I had to keep our dream of life from falling apart. Knowing what has to be done, doesn't always mean you know how to do it. If we are honest, we admit that we are winging it most of the time, especially when it comes to major decisions. Several doctors said Cele's pain might subside on its own, but it didn't. Escape from Mother's painful reality was our only option. Something had to be done. I just didn't know what that option would be or where

I would find it. At the time, I didn't know the answer would find me.

After Cele had "beaten" her cancer, she was still in agony and I was feeling pretty strung out myself. I had already made a commitment to saving Mother. If I were to succeed, I needed to have the time and energy to accomplish my goal. Many months earlier, while Mother was undergoing treatment and before we had been told that the cancer was gone, I had decided to close up my private practice. My plan was to teach at my alma mater, the Texas College of Osteopathic Medicine. They came through and offered me a job teaching Osteopathic Manipulative Treatment as an assistant professor. I accepted. Taking a teaching position was a fiscal and practical move as well. If I left the office in my private practice to attend Mother, my patients wouldn't get the attention they deserved. Also, since my expenses continued whether I was working or not, my income fizzled. As a member of the teaching faculty at the medical school, I would earn a regular salary and share my overhead for rent and staff with others. As a faculty member, I'd also have vacation days in reserve whenever Mother needed me. I informed my employees, began the process of moving my practice to the medical school, and started teaching at the college.

That's how I came to be in the cafeteria at the hospital associated with the school, which was just across the street from the college. I was having lunch there when I happened to run into an anesthesiologist I knew who specialized in pain control. I figured this was no chance meeting. This was a meaningful coincidence. He was just the person I needed at that moment. Here was a man with the options and I could pick his brain. He happily obliged.

He told me about a treatment he could perform that might or might not alleviate my mother's back pain. He added that several treatments might be necessary. Since it doesn't always work on the first try, it could be three months before Cele would know if the procedure had worked at all. The strategy was straightforward—block the impinged nerve pathways emanating from the damaged vertebrae. The procedure would be done in the hospital on an outpatient basis. Mother would receive an injection of lidocaine (which, in some cases, has brought long-lasting relief) into the area causing the pain. The injection was similar to the one Mimi had for her awful back pain before the cancer had been diagnosed.

Since several months had gone by with no relief for Cele and no one was offering any other solutions, I felt we had nothing to lose and recommended the treatment to my mother. She didn't hesitate and went for it. Mother had the first treatment, then her second a month later. Mother was still in pain. As my colleague had said, it turned out that a third treatment would be necessary—another month of waiting for an uncertain outcome. The pain, the chronic coughing and the emotional letdown were combining to form a toxic brew, another depressed state. I felt Mother succumbing. Her energy was just about drained, she was chronically tired and not sleeping. Although it's not unusual for someone in constant pain to become depressed, it's quite another matter when it's someone you love.

I became increasingly worried about Cele. I wasn't sleeping and the thought of her pain was constantly with me. If Mother gave up, she would die. I suggested she see a doctor I knew for osteopathic manipulation treatment (OMT). Mother had gone through a lot. Her primary problem now was dealing with pain—something osteopathic doctors are particularly effective in treating. Mother was game. This doctor's practice focused on a much-in-demand specialty called cranial osteopathy, a noninvasive technique that stimulates the soft tissues, fluids, and nervous system of the body toward achieving a normal state of health.

I made an appointment for the doctor to see Mother before she had her third nerve block. As an osteopathic doctor myself,

I knew firsthand that the benefits of OMT are far-reaching and felt it might relieve the severity of Mother's back pain. I also knew cranial manipulation would help her feel better in general and that would go a long way in lifting her spirits—an incalculably valuable and essential ingredient for healing. At the time, I didn't know that in making this appointment for my mother, submerged and terrifying truths about myself would soon surface. The universe was flowing through us and the tenor of our lives was unstoppable. All we had to do was to show up and make sure we had a sturdy rudder.

Chapter 21

Osteopathic Manipulation

"The human body is a machine run by the unseen force called life, and that it may run harmoniously it is necessary that there be liberty of blood, nerves, and arteries from their generating point to their destination." —A.T. Still

There are many different manipulation treatments in the osteopathic profession and cranial osteopathy is probably the least understood by the public, and by other physicians as well—including DOs and MDs. I learned how to diagnose and treat patients with OMT as a medical student during a comprehensive and demanding two-hundred hour course that had been spread over the first two years of my medical education. In nearly a century of service, osteopathy has improved the lives of thousands of people, including such well-known figures as John D. Rockefeller, Henry Kissinger, former presidents Franklin D. Roosevelt, Dwight D. Eisenhower, John F. Kennedy, and Martina Navratilova.

The cranial concept was originally alluded to by osteopathy's founder, Andrew T. Still, MD (1828–1917). The idea, however, really took form in the early 1900s when it was put forth by William G. Sutherland, DO. Sutherland, whose first professional job was as an investigative reporter for a newspaper, later distinguished himself as an extraordinarily bright medical student and graduated from Kirksville College of Osteopathic Medicine at the age of 25 in 1898. He soon identified that all 26 bones in the skull as being slightly "mobile" and in rhythmic motion. These bones fit together like the intricate gears of a watch that influence each other and they were treatable. This was an outrageous claim at the time. Sutherland was labeled a heretic and a quack. But his insights into the workings of the central nervous system finally began receiving credit in the early 1940s. The treatment involves the application of Dr. Still's principles of osteopathy to the head (cranium) and to the tailbone (sacrum). The cranial osteopath includes these areas in an overall evaluation and treatment plan, considering the whole body as one dynamic, integrated organic machine.

There are many different OMT treatments and variations available that osteopathic physicians can apply in their practice. While everyone in my medical school class was required to take and pass the manipulation courses, not everyone embraced the therapy as their guiding light. Many of my classmates had come to osteopathic medical school because they wanted to become doctors—not because they wanted to or even appreciated the value of becoming a practitioner of osteopathy. This attitude really reflected a simple supply-and-demand situation. In the past, there has been a greater demand for getting into traditional medical schools than schools of osteopathy. Those who had good qualifications but couldn't get in, would most often find acceptance at a less congested medical school of osteopathy. Although much of this balance has changed and equalized in recent years, there are still some who use DO schools as a fallback if they don't get into an MD school.

As for me, I specifically wanted to be an osteopathic physician and I had good reason. Osteopathy had saved my daughter's life and I believed in its holistic approach toward wellness. As a mature med student, I was eager to learn all the OMT treatment modalities. The more I knew, the better off my patients would be. If the majority of my classmates didn't care about the OMT techniques they were required to learn, most cared even less about cranial manipulation. Why care less? Many of my fellow students were intimidated by the school faculty into feeling negatively about this highly beneficial treatment modality. Since the professors teaching cranial osteopathy presented the course as being esoteric and extremely difficult to learn, they left us thinking that few students would ever be able to "feel" or palpate the cranial mechanism successfully. In other words, the message was clear: Most of you aren't going to get it so why bother. Some people buckle when they hear difficulty; others get an adrenaline rush, prepared to make the grade at all costs. Mimi and Cele had taught me to be a member of the latter group.

What osteopathic physicians "feel" is considered by those unfamiliar with the technique as being too vague to be of value, which is an unremarkable perception. The healing power of touch, in a vast array of treatments, has been chronicled for thousands of years in diverse cultures around the world. I kept Mimi's lesson about the nature of thought in mind: Although you can't see a thought, it's as real as gravity. I had developed a theory. The professors at medical school felt cranial osteopathy was hard to teach because the technique was palpable yet subtle—a thing beyond words. You had to feel your way. No internal dialogue. No thinking. Just pure feeling. Just like Mimi's Fudge. I suppose if you set cranial osteopathy up this way, it would be intimidating to students. But not for those dedicated to finding out for themselves.

Before identifying bones in the skull as being slightly "mobile" and treatable was finally accepted within the osteopathic profession, cranial osteopaths were labeled "quacks." Today, it's fairly well established that cranial motion exists and it is central to normal body functions.

Because I could "feel" the cranial mechanism at work while

the vast majority of my classmates could not (just as the professors had predicted), I was one of only two students in my class chosen to instruct the others on the cranial mechanism. Sensing that cranial manipulation would give me a genuine edge in my profession, I was highly motivated to learn this technique. I remembered Mimi's words about her secret for cooking her superb fudge and how you had to feel your way around to get the consistency just right. I was certain my one-on-one cooking course with Master Chef Mimi had been an essential factor for seeing me through medical school with honors.

In my second year of medical school, I was selected by the faculty and other students to become a teaching assistant in the Manipulative Medicine Department. I accepted and helped my fellow classmates get a feel for OMT. When I graduated in 1989, the school presented me with their highest distinction for my achievement in osteopathic manipulation—the Wayne O. Stockseth Award for Osteopathic Excellence. Although the prestigious award was given to me, Mimi and Cele deserve the credit.

Our immune system and nervous system are closely related—you can't have one without the other. In fact, some scientists believe these autonomic systems are one and the same. Even if they're not, it's a moot point. They are wholly dependent on each other to keep the body healthy. We just label them as different systems. We know that both the immune and nervous systems utilize many of the same chemicals such as adrenaline to communicate within the body. We also know that cranial manipulation can stimulate the production of those chemicals, thereby improving the efficiency of the immune and nervous systems.

After all the prodding and invasive therapy Mother had endured, her poor body and psyche needed the gentle healing hands of an experienced cranial osteopath like a doctor I had in mind. Since I didn't think cranial manipulation could cure cancer, I hadn't suggested the treatment during Mother's cancer therapy. This treatment did feel right for her now that the cancer was in full remission. My expectations were that a good cranial manipulation would bolster her debilitated immune system and improve her outlook on life at the same time. Not such a tall order, I thought. Not when I looked back and realized once again that Mother was, despite the sickening aftereffects of poison and burn, miraculously cancer-free. She was going to pull through this thing just fine. I had to maintain the momentum of "making it" for all of us. After all, I was the chief bricklayer building a road toward that realm called health.

Mother had her cranial manipulation with the osteopath. After her treatment, she didn't notice any difference at the time, which is not unusual. There is nothing particularly apparent to the patient on every OMT treatment. If her doctor had been treating her for a headache, the headache would probably have disappeared. But he was working on more subtle issues with Cele. The doctor didn't say much to me at the time. I figured he didn't want to talk shop in front of Mother. We scheduled another appointment and were off.

Will Death Take a Holiday?

A few days later, I ran into the doctor at an OMT meeting. Great, I thought, I'll speak with him when the meeting's over. After the last speaker finished, people began leaving the room. I walked up to the doctor and asked him what he had felt in my mother.

"I have to tell you Mary Ann," he said, "after treating your mother the other day, I feel she's going to die."

While I appreciate directness, his words felt like merciless daggers. I felt mortally wounded, stunned, and temporarily speechless.

Everyone else had already left and we were the only ones left standing in the room. Two doctors face to face. The fear I had been converting into courage with positive thoughts for months didn't fall apart. It exploded. I went ballistic and screamed, "How dare you say that! She's not going to die. The cancer is gone. My mother is going to live!"

The doctor didn't seem surprised by my outburst. He remained unflappable.

I was furious. I couldn't believe my colleague was telling me this horrible news. "How could Mother be dying?" I said. "If the cancer is now truly gone . . . and it is, why wouldn't you tell me she's going to live?" My blood was boiling and my skin was on fire.

He cleared his throat, then said: "Mary Ann, the cancer might be gone, but what I felt while treating your mother was that death was very near. Her vitality is gone. Your mother doesn't have the energy left to live."

Oh my God, I thought. Here I was again. I remembered when, months ago or ages ago it seemed, Mother's doctor had come into the postoperative room of the hospital where Daddy and I were waiting in our vigil. I remembered thinking, here it comes, be ready for whatever it is. "I'm sorry," said Mother's doctor, "she has lung cancer." His words fell on me like an ax, hacking my world into pieces. Now, this doctor's words felt like that same ax coming at me once again—this time for the kill.

I began crying hysterically. I was caught off guard, totally unprepared for such dire news. The carefully woven rug of hope I had been weaving for Mother had been pulled out from under me. No longer grounded in my reality, I felt myself falling into an abyss. I was afraid. I knew what he was saying could be true. I knew my mother was terribly weak. There were scary times when I'd stop over at her house. She'd answer the door, her limp body looking as lifeless as a worn out washrag. I'd smile, trying not to let on how I felt. Cele was certainly not her old self—

very far from it. I was reminded again that this life was a play. Dying after you've won the battle would be the anticlimax—a weak ending to a strong finish. Had all that hard work fighting the cancer been for nothing? I couldn't stand it. I was devastated by the doctor's prognosis. Holding together is hard when everything inside you wants to collapse into a heap of irresponsible disappointment.

Afraid that he might be right, I continued arguing the issue with him. I wanted nothing to shatter my reality, which was developing serious hairline cracks. Despite my respect for this osteopath, I refused to believe that my mother was going to die after we had defeated the cancer. Just when I felt my test of faith in the power of positive thinking was finally over, it was starting all over again. Would the tests ever end, I wondered?

I didn't become hysterical without good reason. This doctor was no slouch. He knew what he was talking about. When he told me he felt my mother was going to die, I knew he had felt it on a subtle level most people cannot appreciate. In fact, first-time patients are usually surprised by what a cranial osteopath can feel with the ancient diagnostic and healing technology called touch.

A skilled osteopath can feel the essence of a person through her hands. This is not hearsay. I know. As an osteopath, I can sense it, too. I can feel the level of vitality within a patient streaming through my hands. Let me give you a couple of examples that illustrate the point. An osteopathic colleague of mine walked into a room to treat a 45-year-old woman patient. He put one hand on her head and said: "When you were seven years old you fell off a swing backwards, landed on your head and twisted your right leg." With wide-eyed amazement, the woman responded, "How did you know?" There was another instance when I watched an osteopathic doctor put his hand on the arm of a new patient and say, "When you were thirteen you were sexually abused." The patient was shocked and indicated the doctor was accurate. While these cases may sound like parlor tricks seen on afternoon TV talk shows, they most certainly are not. These instances exemplify the depth of feeling comprehension and healing an osteopathic physician can bring to her profession—which, to this day, is still a revelation to most people.

There had to be something inside my mother that had sent the doctor a message that death was just around the corner. My grandmother had taught me that you must rely on yourself. Memories of Mimi were speaking to me during these interminably long and stressful days. Still, as much as I respected my osteopath colleague, I wasn't about to accept his impressions as being carved in stone. His feeling was only one future possibility. We could still act. We could still head off death at the pass. Just as I rejected the grim prognosis by the conventional doctors of my mother's terminal illness, I certainly wasn't about to accept her dying now that the cancer was gone.

My hysteria must have been more intense than I thought. The doctor offered to give me a cranial treatment right there on the spot in the meeting room to help me calm down. I don't know what he expected when he told me my mother would surely die. How can you overreact to that? In retrospect, his timing was impeccable. He had told me precisely the right thing about Mother.

"You could really use a somato-emotional release treatment," he said, pointing to one of the manipulation tables in the meeting room.

I agreed, nodding a big yes. I was spent and could barely talk.

"Somato" refers to the body. Using cranial manipulation, an osteopath can trigger a somato-emotional release that allows a patient to experience intense feelings lying below the surface of awareness. The doctor thought it would be useful if he could help me get to the undercurrent that was driving my emotions about Cele. Suddenly, I had become the patient. Perhaps he saw my hysteria and unwillingness to accept my mother's fate as a form of denial. Somato-emotional release is an effective process.

Eyes Wide Opened

I lay down on the manipulation table on my back, with my eyes closed. He placed his hands under my head just above the neck. To the casual observer, it may appear as if nothing is happening since no conspicuous movement is taking place. For the patient, it's a whole other matter. While treating me, he began talking about my mother, about the manipulation he had given her, and how I felt about it all. My head felt like a piece of lead that had been dropped into an ocean. Down, down, down. I felt paralyzed as I drifted into an abyss I had felt before. Then, in a flash, memory-linked neurons, feelings and thoughts, collided with a primal bang within my very core. My body became an organic high energy particle accelerator, like those used to discover the identity, properties, and purpose of minute particles that make up the universe. Instead of subatomic quarks, bosons, or leptons colliding, the particles exposed in my reality shook the foundation of my sense of self, my sense of purpose. A thing doesn't exist for the viewer until it's seen, and our range of vision is so narrow.

Images streamed at an incredible rate across the movie screen of my life. They were moving so quickly, I had to grab for one as the others rushed past me and faded in the distance. There was my long-departed dog, my dear Pompom, running toward me in that cute, awkward puppy gait. I tried reaching for her, but she ran right through me as if I were a ghost. Then, I saw myself at 10 years old with Mimi who seemed to be a girl about my own age. How can this be? I thought. We were both on her pony, Sugar, riding along a trail in the deep forest. It was early morning and the air was brisk. I sat on the saddle behind cowgirl Mimi with my arms around her waist. In a girlish voice, Mimi told me that she was taking me to see something special, something important. It was just over the next ridge. Sugar moved forward steadily, his hooves muffled in the moist, soft earth, his nostrils blowing mist into the chilled air. Just as Mimi and I were about to reach the summit of the hill, I vanished, only to reappear as a teenager in the crowded hallway of my high school. I was checking my locker to make sure my pack of cigarettes was still there. I had a crush on a boy named Jimmy. I had decided I'd start smoking to impress him. I went outside and hid from view. I pulled out a cigarette, lit up, and took a deep drag. I started coughing a bit, but I was getting the knack. I'm alone, speechless, and breathless. I'm floating away again. My body is shaking uncontrollably—like a shiver that won't stop.

Then, suddenly, quiet motion. I'm weightless, flying, rising toward the surface, up from the deep toward air, toward resolution, toward the underlying truth I had for wanting my mother to live that seemed almost treacherous. The somato-emotional release session had done its work.

Chapter 22

Truth of the Matter

"How hard it is sometimes to trust the evidence of one's senses!
How reluctantly the mind consents to reality!"
—Norman Douglas

As soon as I got home, I called Joni. She came right over. Buried in the far recesses of my subconscious was a selfish reason driving me to beat Mother's cancer at all costs. When Cele was seeing Dr. Craselneck, she didn't become aware that her subconscious mind saw only one lonely white blood cell surrounded by a swarming army of cancer cells until he had hypnotized her. Knowing how she really felt allowed her to more fully mobilize against the cancer on a conscious level. In much the same way, the somato-emotional release brought a truth to the surface—my subconscious mind didn't want my mother to die because I was terrified of what that meant for me.

I told Joni. "My mother's pretty depressed and I'm not feeling so hot either. I'm worried. She could die on us. It's not good."

"Can I help?" said Joni. "Just tell me."

"Thanks, I wish there was something you could do." I fell silent.

"I found out something disturbing about myself," I said. "It's really been twisting around inside me, like a corkscrew trying to punch its way out of me."

"You know how I've poured myself into saving my mother?" I said.

Nodding her head, Joni's eyes said, yes, we know this to be so.

"My undying devotion to my mother has been self-serving," I said. "My motives have been less than benevolent."

"What is it?" said Joni. "You're talking around whatever it is that's got you spooked."

"The truth of the matter is that I was driven by unseen forces to save my mother. Mother's death meant I would follow her on 'death row.' I was driven by fear, not by pure compassion. I've been deceiving myself."

Driven by fear. We all have feelings and thoughts we'd rather not have, let alone admit to. I realized this was one of those rare times when you get a chance to see yourself as you really are, not a mirror image dressed up by the ego. I remembered what Rosalind Russell, the actress, said: "Acting is standing up naked and turning around very slowly." That just how I felt.

"Mary Ann," said Joni. "Is this the confession, the revelation that's got you by the tail? You worked hard to save your mother to prove that you wouldn't die . . . is that it?"

"Unconsciously, I felt that if I could prevent my mother from dying of lung cancer then I wouldn't die from it either. I was thinking about number one first."

Joni's eyes focused forward, giving her a serious look. "And what's wrong with that, I'd like to know? If you don't take care of number one, there is no number two. That's what you've always told me. Remember, 'If you don't take care of yourself, you won't be healthy enough to take care of anyone else.' I believe that is a Mary Ann Block truism."

"You remember I told you that my grandmother and my father's brother, Bill, died of lung cancer."

Joni nodded.

"And now Mother just had it, too."

"So?"

"I got to thinking what if all the women and some of the men in my family tree were genetically predisposed to lung cancer."

"I see," said Joni. Now it's making sense.

"But this wasn't something I was aware of."

"Well, now that we know you're definitely not a saint, it seems the end did justify the means. Your mother's alive and you proved the doctors wrong. What a coup. What a statement. You proved that the impossible can be done," added Joni.

"I know you'll soon transform this 'painful' revelation into something creative and positive. I'm sure of it. And if giving Cele life didn't come from the pure place you feel is so important, then you've got more work to do. Doesn't she need you now?" said Joni.

"Yes, Joni, you're absolutely right. I feel something brewing."

"What?"

"I'm not sure just yet." I sat back and took a deep breath, grateful to have Joni as my sounding board. Suddenly, the whole somato-emotional thing was starting to take a direction inside my head.

I took stock. There had to be a flip side in this universe of duality. Although my own survival wasn't the only reason I wanted my mother to live, it had raised its foreboding head as a fundamental reason during my somatic-emotional release. It certainly explained my severe panic attack when the doctor told me Mother was going to die. It was clear to me now. My unconscious heard his words as: "Mary Ann is going to die." Now that I was facing myself in full frontal honesty, I understood self-preservation had to come first if I was going to be of value for my family. The cards were on the table. We were still in the game. Time to ante up again, Mary Ann, I thought to myself. I also remembered not to play against the house. I was making it up as I went along.

Hearing that Mother was on her last legs and learning that my motivation was not wholly benevolent was a huge wake-up call. The doctor had snapped me out of my lethargy of feeling safe and victorious. My anger at him and myself was waning. I had more work to do.

My perspective of the somato-emotional release experience had widened after my talk with Joni. I had already formulated a plan of action. I called Dr. Jordan. I brought him up to speed on how poorly Mother was doing. I told him how she was in pain, felt depressed, and had no energy. I kept the osteopath's prediction about Mother to myself. He listened patiently. For Dr. Jordan and his associate, Dr. Friess, their mission had been successfully completed—Mother's cancer was gone.

Dr. Jordan said, "It's not that unusual. I know it sounds strange, Mary Ann, but I've seen patients die after their cancer had gone into remission."

"Why?" I said, waiting for the other slipper to drop.

"Well," he said, "there does appear to be a pattern. These deaths did seem to occur as a direct result of a deep depression."

Bingo! It hit me. There's more to life than avoiding death. We needed more than medicine. My heart jumped. It was true. The oncologist confirmed what my osteopathic colleague had told me. Mother could die with the cancer in remission. I had to act and act fast. I had to alter my mother's thought process away from depression and pull her back from the outstretched arms of death. I had to reach her first. I had to put her back on that magic yellow brick road I had been building. The enchanted Land of Oz beckoned as I always knew it would. This time I was ready to pull up all emotional stakes and make the move. All we needed to succeed was all too familiar and all too rare: brains, courage, and heart. Mother had all those qualities.

I had become lax after seeing Mother's cancer-free X ray in Dr. Jordan's office. I had been wrong—dead wrong. Just because the cancer was gone didn't mean we were home free—at least, not yet. I had to get us through this next phase of healing. This wasn't a delusion or some tenuous co-dependency issue. This was a matter of doing what you have to do for your mother. Her body and spirit had been decimated. She had given the fight of her life; she had won the battle but she was about to lose the war. I wasn't going to let that happen. While I might have considered myself her cheerleader before, now I had to be her team with the strength and talent to support a winning season. If we were able to rid Mother of the cancer, we would find a way of returning her to emotional health.

I had to have a talk with Mother. We were in her bedroom, she in her chair and I sitting on the bed. Daddy was in the room listening intently. I was excited. I felt I had finally figured out what was really wrong. And now that it was identified, properly diagnosed, I knew I could fix it. I explained to Cele that the chemotherapy and radiation had damaged her body physically and the very nature of her battle with the cancer had depleted her emotional energy. She didn't realize this had happened to her on a conscious level. She had to hear the healing words of awareness from me. When you feel that bad, it's not a stretch to think you're still dying.

What Cele did not know could kill her—yet another exception to my don't tell Cele rule. I laid it on the line. "Mother," I said, "even though the cancer's gone, you could still die from the secondary aftereffects. I know you've fought hard. Now, you've got to fight even harder. I know you feel wasted. I know you feel you've had it. I know you feel emotionally and physically drained. I also know that you've got to dig deeper inside yourself. I know there's more strength waiting to be tapped. You taught me these values. And now I'm giving them back to you."

Everyone can use a pep talk. This one sure sounded like one more for the gipper from an old Ronald Reagan film about football.

Mother readily accepted what I said and was ready to do

whatever was necessary. Cele is a very logical individual. My talk made sense to her and that was the key that launched us in a positive direction once again.

We had to make a concerted all-out effort if Mother was going to win. We were so close I could smell the sweet aroma of victory. After all, I had become a physician to protect my family. Happily, my concerns were short-lived. Three months after Cele's remission, when I began teaching at the medical school, my mother was doing great. She was still in pain, but her outlook was beautiful. I knew she had a strong desire to live. The simple act of understanding why she was feeling badly after becoming cancer-free had been just the tonic to overcome her depression.

Mother finally went in for nerve block number three. We didn't know whether or not this treatment was going to ultimately work. Daddy and I were in the hospital anxiously waiting for her. The third time was the charm. A few days after the procedure, when the pain of the treatment itself wore off, my mother was both cancer- and pain-free. This was a glorious eternal moment in our lives. For the first time in months, I felt I could finally breathe. Cele felt ready to move forward and put some degree of normalcy back into her life. She wanted to start living again. Although she had been visualizing a future throughout her illness, she could now begin to live one. A miracle had fallen into our laps and we accepted it graciously.

Cele wasted no time. After her final nerve block had healed, she and Daddy made reservations for an ocean cruise. I remembered our stay at the M.D. Anderson Cancer Center and how I tried to get our minds off Mother's cancer by suggesting we make believe we were on a cruise. Although my role-playing maneuver about being passengers bound for some exotic isle hadn't worked too well months earlier, it had now manifested itself into the real thing. The power of thought humbled me. Patience was the ingredient to see things through.

Chapter 23

The Unsinkable Cele Ritzwoller

"I remember some months after Cele had been diagnosed with lung cancer, I saw her and her husband, Dave, at the bank. I was making a quick transaction and stopped for a moment to say hello. She was thin, drawn, and looked sick—as if she was dying. I couldn't help but notice that they were revising their wills. Later that day, I called Mary Ann and mentioned that I had seen Cele updating her will and how sad I felt. Mary Ann dismissed my concern in a serene voice, saying: 'Joni, there's no problem. She's 75 years old. It's perfectly normal for my mother and father to make sure their affairs are in order. It's the responsible thing to do.' I remember getting off the phone thinking how single-minded Mary Ann had been through unimaginable depths of adversity. Her unwavering belief that Cele was going to be O.K. had ultimately paved the road, brick by brick, for her mother, for us all, to follow." —Joan Anderson

With Mother being in "complete and total remission" for nearly a decade, I never forget that she has had cancer twice. Every three months she sees Dr. Jordan for an X ray; she also gets a CT or bone scan on a rotating basis each year as well. After the tests are done, my mother calls me. I'm impatient and can't wait for her doctor to get the radiologist's findings and then tell us about it. This process is far too slow for my temperament. I wrap up whatever I'm doing as quickly as possible, drive over to the hospital, and make a beeline for the radiologist on duty. The doctor graciously grants me a professional courtesy and lets me look over his shoulder while he reads Mother's X ray.

Over the years, rushing off to the hospital and getting the x-ray result "hot off the press" has turned into a ritual for me. When the radiologist tells me "No change," I sigh a sigh of relief. We enjoy the good news together, then I rush off for the nearest phone and call Cele. Reassuring my mother that her cancer is, in fact, still gone, warms my heart and reassures my unconscious that all is well with me. After a couple of weeks, I receive the official radiology report from Dr. Jordan. I always re-read the part that shouts "Complete and total remission" and take a special moment to revel in our victory over circumstance.

Each time Mother has an X ray or scan, we reach back a little further into our reality with a little more fervor. We replace any apprehension, fear, or doubt with our own vision and a grasp that's a little more tractable. We let the light of our dreams surround us and we bathe in its comfort. Despite ten years and thirty-six reassuring X rays and scans, we never take these tests for granted. Our duty is never done and this is true for any goal that we set for ourselves. We must work toward them and then work harder to maintain and transcend them. In life, you're either moving backward or forward. You can tread water only for so long.

These past ten years have been spectacular—nearly a decade that the doctors, who had given up on my mother, who didn't know any better, would have denied her. I'm ecstatic over what my mother has lived to witness. She has celebrated her 84th birthday; she has seen her children grow and blossom into their fifties; she has seen her three granddaughters marry; she has seen Randy graduate from college and law school; she has celebrated her 60th wedding anniversary with Daddy; she has held her first great-grandchild, Paige, in her loving arms—truly, anything is possible.

Mother and Daddy have left their footprints in Europe, the

Orient, Canada, and places throughout the United States. Despite this active pace, Daddy, who's approaching his 94th year, has the stamina of a much younger man. He needs it to keep up with Mother. He drives, takes care of the bills, reads several books a week, learns new technology, sends E-mail, bought a satellite dish, and works in the yard.

In the birthday category, the highlight had been my father's 90th in 1997—a milestone by any reckoning. The family gathered in Fort Worth for a lovely private dinner where we played games, including a special edition of "Jeopardy" that I had constructed expressly for Daddy. I prepared the board game with cards containing answers about my father's life experiences. Daddy, as in the real game, had to guess the questions. His keen memory served him well. He won the game about his own life, sharing anecdotes about events as he went along. His memory did fail him when we viewed slides of the family taken on Mother's Day, 1991. One slide seemingly stumped him.

"Who's that woman there, sitting next to me?" my father asked in all seriousness.

As the slide came into focus, there, sitting in the middle of the couch with all the family around her was Mother—frail, bone thin, wearing her blond wig that now looked much too big for her drawn face. And Daddy did not recognize her.

We all laughed. Yes, I thought, the Hollywood formula does make sense now. Pain plus time does eventually equal humor.

In the midst of the merrymaking, I took a quiet moment to reflect. I could still remember, in vivid detail, the way Mimi looked with cancer because those are my last memories of her. As amazing as it sounds, Daddy didn't remember Mother with cancer. His recent memories of her as a healthy woman had completely displaced that brief harrowing period when Mother had been fighting for her life. By not recognizing the way his own wife looked when she had cancer, Daddy was not only living our reality, he was unconsciously reinforcing it.

Mother continues to play cards with her group twice a week. Being a creative and independent soul, she also thrives on solo activities. She's sewed "couturier" clothing and has worked with the arts all her life, and continues to do so. When I think of all the wonderful things my mother did for me, I always come back to the memory of when I was a tiny 13-year-old girl who couldn't find clothes that fit, and how Mother would sketch the clothes I liked and custom tailor my childhood finery. My mother had loved me through all my ups and downs. To have helped Mother win her life back went beyond marvelous.

Recently, Cele surprised everyone by taking up painting—she's done some wonderful landscape and abstract work. Her talent as an artist is remarkable, yet not altogether surprising, given her lifelong flair for improvisation and working with her nimble hands. All her grandchildren have put in orders to have Cele's artwork grace the walls of their homes. I'm last on the list and very eager to receive mine. I don't mind waiting. Mother has the luxury of time to spend these days.

Randy Makes the Grade

Since Cele had used Randy's future wedding as her visualization for living, it was really no surprise that nothing would keep her from attending my son's graduation from Rice University, which took place on a hot June day in 1995. Undaunted by distance or heat, my parents drove to Houston for the commencement. To keep cool, Mother, Daddy, Steve, Gail, Stan, Cathy, and I sat under the shade of a large oak tree during the graduation. As Randy was nearing the podium, Mother suddenly jumped up, grabbed her camera, and rushed up to the platform. Nothing was going to prevent her from getting in on this photo-op. She waited under the blistering Texas sun to snap a photo of

Randy accepting his diploma. Although the heat had already sapped most of us into limpness, Mother and Daddy took an active part in the celebration festivities that followed.

Three years later, my parents attended Randy's graduation from Southern Methodist University Law School (SMU). Mother not only braved the Texas heat again, she withstood the added difficulty of breathing in the toxic smoke in the air caused by out-of-control fires blowing northward from Mexico. Although Cele's lungs were damaged from the radiation, her spirit had remained intact. Cele never complained. If cancer couldn't keep her from seeing Randy graduate from college, neither would environmental hazards prevent her from seeing her grandson receive his law degree. I'm sure Mother was thinking that the next big event for Randy would be his wedding and she was already planning what she'd wear.

My parents have been on more long trips and short jaunts than most people their age. In the past ten years, their well-traveled suitcases have barely been stored away. They are in a perpetual motion process of planning a trip, shopping for a trip, or going on a trip. In July 1991, after Mother's cancer had gone into remission, she and Daddy went for a weeklong trek into the Canadian Rockies with my brother, Steve and his wife, Gail.

My brother described one day's adventure on a mountain with my indomitable Mother.

"The four of us were driving around seeing the sights in the Canadian Rockies on one of our daily jaunts. Mother, 75 years old at the time, was reading a guide book that described a beautiful waterfall nearby. We decided to have a look and drove to the spot in the forest indicated on the map. We parked. No falls in sight. We discovered the waterfall was actually down a trail along a river about a mile away. It was early in the day and we all felt good. The crisp

Canadian air was wonderful and invigorating. Mother was up for it so our little expedition headed out and down. The trail was narrow and at times tricky as it hugged the edge of the path that overlooked a dizzying drop to the river below. About halfway down, Daddy got tired and decided to wait on a bench while we went on. Mother was feeling the strain, but she was determined to make it. We continued and eventually reached the magnificent falls, the sight made all the more grand because Mother didn't give up. Afterwards, we began our way back, picked up Daddy, and made it back up the mountain."

Steve's simple story brought more tears to this doctor's eyes. I wouldn't expect less from Mother. After all, she had Mimi's pioneer spirit flowing through her brave veins.

Mother's lung cancer had been an awful, gut-wrenching ordeal. For Cele, words are inadequate to describe the experience. I remember one of my lessons from Mimi. It's essential to make the most of what you do have, to make gold out of straw with a heart full of gratitude and generosity—a concept that all too often eludes us in a society where more never seems to be quite enough. Mother's illness had reminded us to appreciate the precious moments of our lives together. We paid attention to Cele's pain and triumph, and our family ties have become stronger with the passing years.

Cele lived through the dark day of her diagnosis, her depression after her remission, and has prevailed despite the very real potential for disaster looming over her head every day. Cele has risen to the top—a survivor as buoyant as the legendary unsinkable Molly Brown of *Titanic* fame. Cele Ritzwoller didn't have a model for dying, so she didn't.

Epilogue

"This is the true joy in life, the being used for a purpose recognized by yourself as a mighty one." —George Bernard Shaw

A few years ago I asked my mother what she felt was the key to conquering her lung cancer. She had undergone chemotherapy, radiation, and a multitude of alternative treatments, including nutritional and immunological therapies. She had taken nutrients orally, intravenously and through injections. She had been hypnotized and had walked down her private path with guided imagery as her companion. Was there a treatment, or some combination, that had made the difference?

Mother thought for a moment, then said, "I wouldn't have skipped any of them because we'll never truly know if any single treatment deserves the credit. It was probably all of them together."

I had to agree. It was a combined effort of protocols, timing, and her outlook on life that had won the day.

Several years ago, my mother wrote me a letter thanking me for saving her life. Here it is:

Dear Mary Ann,

I am so proud of all you have accomplished and for staying so close and giving me two wonderful grandchildren, so on this Mother's Day I want to thank you for being my daughter and saving my life. I couldn't have done it without you.

Love, Mother

While she gives me the credit, she's the one who saved her-self. I provided her with the tools. She did all the hard work to stay in this life. She suffered through the brutal chemotherapy and radiation, through nausea and wrenching vomiting, through hair loss, weakness, and agony. She's the one who swallowed all the vitamins and minerals, took the shots and IVs, and read all the books. She's the one who endured the daily unrelenting or-deal of pain and dreaded uncertainty.

Reading Mother's letter brought back memories of years ago when she was undergoing the throes of treatment for the can-cer. I remembered that there was one thing my mother hadn't told me about, a thing I had discovered on my own, a scene for-ever etched in my heart. Mother had endured a chemotherapy treatment the day before and I had come over quite early in the morning to see how she was doing. I walked into their home to find Daddy already in the kitchen. He pointed toward the hall. I moved quietly toward the bedroom. The door was half open.

I said, "Mother?"

Only a light muffled sound of someone speaking.

I entered the room. I moved toward the light and muted speech coming from the bathroom. I was so quiet I don't think that I was even breathing. The door was slightly ajar. I put one eye to the crack and looked through. From the opening, I had a clear view of my remarkable mother. In spite of her ravaged body, she continued to stand strong in the reality of her own making, her own choosing. I could see that she was eyeing her frail reflection in the medicine cabinet mirror. Then, I heard her repeat out loud what had been unclear a moment ago. With tenacity and in overt defiance of the cancer, she said, "Today . . . I . . . will . . . not . . . die!   Today . . . I . . . will . . . not . . . die!"

I backed out of the room undetected, leaving Cele with her private moment, knowing now the magic words she used each day to face the demons of cancer. I went into the kitchen with Daddy, felt Mimi's ring on one hand, mother's ring on the other, and waited for our future to unfold.

PART TWO

TAKING ACTION

Taking Action

In this section, I describe the protocol I developed to help my mother become cancer-free. In addition, you will find information about cancer and the different treatment options that are available. Last but not least, you will find lists of valuable resources, including books, Web sites, recommended supplement companies and other products that can help you to protect yourself and your loved ones against cancer.

Cele's Protocol
The Enemy Within
Is Your Biology Your Destiny?
Another World
Smoking: Puff, The Not-So-Magic Dragon
Web Sites
Bibliography
Recommended Reading
Publisher's Resource Guide

Cele's Protocol

"I had an immense advantage over many others dealing with the problem inasmuch as I had no fixed ideas derived from long-established practice to control and bias my mind, and did not suffer from the general belief that whatever is, is right." —Henry Bessemer, discoverer of a new method of producing steel

When my grandmother was diagnosed with lung cancer in 1972, I became an American Cancer Society (ACS) volunteer. Back then you would never find anything in their newsletter about nutrition and cancer. Nearly twenty years later, when my mother learned she had lung cancer, the newsletter had begun mentioning nutritional treatments, from vitamins to green tea. I'm glad to see that the focus of the newsletter has become more progressive. Today, the ACS offers an expanded list of complementary approaches such as: art therapy, biofeedback, garlic, herbal teas, massage therapy, meditation, music therapy, prayer, spiritual practices, t'ai chi, and yoga.

Times have changed, and so has our knowledge base. More information on cancer treatment is published in the medical literature on a regular basis. Although many oncologists don't have the time or inclination to check out all the late-breaking news in the medical literature, they need to know that there is a great deal more to treating cancer besides chemotherapy, radiation, and surgery. At the very least, doctors need to be supportive of alternative and complementary approaches, especially if the patient is facing certain death. The cure for cancer is still around that cagey corner. Until then, if a treatment won't hurt and might help, let's try it. This is still my philosophy.

All the nutritional supplements that my mother took then, she still takes to this day. Both she and I know that it is easier to prevent a disease than to cure it. There is supporting documentation in the medical literature for everything used to treat my mother's cancer: I know because I researched it personally. My decisions were based on studies, some small, some large. If something appeared to help fight cancer, I included it. If something seemed to encourage cancer, I excluded it.

I think this should be done at the outset, from the day of the diagnosis. I have seen patients whose doctors, having failed at their attempts to help the patient through conventional means, tell them, "I've done all I can do. You can try alternative treatments now." Why wait until the cancer has progressed to offer this suggestion? I believe that starting with all of these treatments at the onset of my mother's cancer treatment program allowed both the conventional and the complementary treatments to have the best results. No one had survived as long as my mother has using only the conventional treatments. But the radiation and chemotherapy were very important in "knocking down" the cancer. Once down, I believe the complementary treatments helped my mother overcome and conquer. After all, why not give everyone every opportunity for success?

Here you will find the protocol I used to help save my mother from terminal lung cancer nearly a decade ago. Since then, I've come across new options, which I would include if I were treating my mother today. A new protocol is preceded by a **new** label.

Traditional Treatment

Radiation and chemotherapy were administered to my mother concurrently based on a protocol devised by Dr. Gregg Friess. At the time, no one else was combining radiation and chemotherapy together for this type of lung cancer. The mainstream approach offered palliative radiation only.

Radiation Treatment

Shrinking field technique using multiple ports. Supraclavicular area, right upper lobe, right hilum and adjacent mediastanum were given 3780 cGy at 180 cGy per treatment. Followed by treatment through lateral opposed ports to the primary area, adjacent right hilum and mediastinum for an additional 900 cGy through lateral opposed customized ports. An additional 900 cGy through the opposed ports to the right hilar area and adjacent mediastinum.

Chemotherapy Treatment

Combination of cisplatin, 50 mg/m IV on days 1 and 8 and etoposide, 50 mg/m IV on days 1 to 5. Chemotherapy was repeated at 28 day intervals during radiotherapy. Two courses of chemotherapy were given during radiotherapy with a third after completion. A fourth round of chemo was planned but proved to be unnecessary.

Complementary Treatments

"When a white-tailed deer was hurt, a vet cleaned the wounded area with carbolic water and bandaged it. The deer darted away, pulled the bandage off, licked the wound, exposed it to the sunlight, and healed himself."   —Erma Bombeck

I recommend locating a physician who is trained in and understands the importance of nutrition to help with nutritional supplementation.

Nutritional Supplements Taken Orally

Magnesium
500 mg
Twice per day as magnesium glycinate, citrate, or aspartate

Vitamin E
400 IU/day
This supplement was not used until the chemotherapy was completed because the oncologist informed us that vitamin E could actually interfere with my mother's particular form of chemotherapy.

Selenium
200 mcg/day

Beta-Carotene
30,000–60,000 IU/day

Zinc
30 mg/day

Evening Primrose Oil
500 mg/day

Fish oil-
Max EPA
Fish oil can be taken orally. If, however, the taste is objectionable to you, the oil can work externally by applying it directly to any part of the skin. I recommended that my mother rub the oil over her stomach area or feet.

Vitamin D
400 IU/day

Vitamin K
300 mcg/day

Vitamin B$_{12}$
sublingual (under the tongue)

Multivitamin
with all the B vitamins included

Multi-mineral
given at different time of day from multivitamin

Vitamin C
to bowel tolerance
As much as can be taken without getting loose stools. In Mother's case, 10–12 g+. Individuals with kidney problems must use less and should consult physician for amounts.

Lactobacillus acidophilus and Bifidus (dairy-free)
1 capsule or ½ teaspoon 3 times/day of each

Niacin
1.5 gr/day

Garlic capsules 1–2 times per day

Vitamins and Minerals Administered through IV twice weekly

Magnesium ($MgSo_4$)
50% solution, 8 ml

Chromium, 20 mcg/ml, 10ml

B complex
3 ml

Zinc
1 mg/ml, 1ml

Manganese
200 mg/ml, 1 ml

Saline
0.45 normal, 250 ml

new: Vitamin C
10 g

Dietary Changes

Yes	No
Green/yellow vegetables: broccoli cauliflower, Brussels sprouts	Sugar
Decreased protein	Cow's milk dairy (milk, cheese, yogurt)
Low fat foods	Alcohol
Pau d'arco tea (several cups daily)	Cured or pickled foods (sandwich meats, hot dogs, pickles)
New: Soybean products (such as tofu)	Iron supplements
New: Green tea	

Injections

Twice weekly

Magnesium sulfate
50% solution, 2 cc

Pyridoxine HCcl (vitamin B$_6$)
100 mg/ml 1cc

Lidocaine
2% 1 cc
Magnesium, pyridoxine, and lidocaine were all combined in one injection and given deep IM, "Z" track with a 23-Gauge 1½" needle. This size needle is imperative to adequately reach the muscle and dispense the magnesium with the least discomfort.

Biopharmacotherapy

The concept of this protocol was based on utilizing biological materials that encompassed both natural substances and drugs. The goals of this approach would provide the body with what it needed to help build up the immune system so the body's own agents could fight the cancer itself.

Cimetidine
300 mg four times per day
One side effect of this drug is that it lowers the white cell count. Since chemotherapy already destroys white cells in vast numbers, we used cimetidine with caution. After taking this medication for several weeks, Mother stopped because her white bloods cells were dropping dangerously low as was noted on the contraindication.

Indomethacin
50 mg four times per day after food
This drug can irritate the stomach the same way aspirin does.

Butyrate
8–10 g four times per day

Staphage lysate
1 cc ampoule
Started at 0.15 cc given subcutaneously. Dose was increased or decreased by 0.05 cc every other day until there was an area of growth or redness approximately 50 mm in diameter at the injection site. Staphage lysate is now only available from veterinarians. It took several weeks for my mother to reach the 50 mm skin reaction. When she reached the desired threshold, she appeared noticeably improved.

Hypnosis and Guided Imagery

There is no question in my mind that positive thinking was essential in saving my mother. Hypnosis sessions with qualified practitioners and guided imagery tapes helped my mother keep her focus when times got really tough. People succeed because they believe they can. The best candidates for hypnosis are those who want to be hypnotized and expect to be hypnotized. The best hypnotic subjects are intelligent and without mental impairment.

Medical research into the chemical links among the body systems has produced one of the more intriguing recent theories regarding the suggestive power of hypnosis, which may be mediated by the immune system and other chemically linked autonomic systems, rather than the brain alone. Although a two-way chemical feedback loop has been discovered that operates between the nervous and immune systems, it will take further research to determine its relationship to suggestibility and healing in general. There is, however, basic agreement among most researchers in the field that the "hypnotic state" can consistently produce unusual feats of attention, control, perception, and cognitive dissociation in some subjects. It is important to find a reputable individual to work with you with guided imagery or hypnosis.

Vitamins and Minerals

Vitamins and minerals are essential as cofactors in our biochemical processes. Vitamins are organic compounds that help our bodies use food to supply energy, regulate metabolism and other important functions. There are two categories of vitamins: oil-soluble and water-soluble. The water-soluble vitamins B complex, C, and the bioflavonoids need to be replenished daily as they are not stored in the body. Oil-soluble vitamins A, D, E, and K are absorbed and build up in body tissue. It should be noted that oil-soluble vitamins can be harmful if too much is stored in the body. Minerals are the building materials for bones, teeth, tissue, muscle, blood, and nerve cells.

If we don't have these cofactors in our system, then our bodies will not function properly. Obtaining these nutritional supplements exclusively from the average American diet, which is a disaster for the most part, is difficult, risky, and most likely impossible. It's been demonstrated that processed grocery store bought food doesn't contain the same level of nutrition found in organic foods. For this reason, taking the necessary nutritional supplements and dosage is a must to insure that our bodies maintain an optimum immune system—our most important line of defense.

Drugs Are Not Nutrients

Unlike nutrients, drugs cannot be evaluated in the same manner since they are not naturally found in our bodies. While nutrients are part of every biochemical process that takes place in the complex organic machine that is the body, this is not true of drugs, which are most often manufactured chemicals that are foreign to the body. Drugs rarely cure anything. My mother's doctor told us that the goal of chemotherapy, which is highly toxic, was to kill the cancer before killing her. Nutrients are not toxic and our bodies know precisely how to utilize each of them.

Although nutrients must work together, there have been many studies that have attempted to isolate and evaluate nutrients as independent factors to determine their efficacy upon the body—as if they behaved like lone drugs. Studies of individual nutrients can't reflect accurate holistic results since supplements, like everything else in the universe, work synergistically. While many of these studies included only one nutrient at a time and did, in fact, show benefits in their sole use, it is important that we keep in mind that each and every one of us is biochemically unique. You don't want to live your life according to the FDA's recommended daily allowance (RDA) scheme for the average person. Our biochemical individuality determines the proper dosage of each nutrient we need. The "drug" model of testing one supplement at a time to see if it works for a specific disease entity will not work when we are trying to determine which vitamin, mineral, or other nutrient may be beneficial in preventing or treating cancer.

To establish which nutrients and in what combinations and levels are needed to help counteract cancer, we'll need large studies that will first test each patient for such deficiencies. The current RDA is inadequate; these recommended minimum amounts are adequate in preventing such diseases as scurvy (vitamin C deficiency) and rickets (vitamin D deficiency). Treating and preventing cancer is much more complex than taking a multiple vitamin. Until doctors are educated in nutrition, complementary approaches, and alternative protocols, I don't believe we will see a significant shift in our cancer statistics.

Beta-Carotene

Dr. Richard Shekelle of The University of Texas Health Science Center of Houston, found that men who consumed at least 5,000 IU of beta-carotene per day had the lowest risk of developing lung cancer; for men who rarely ate foods rich in beta-carotene, the risk increased by 48 percent. In a study of 3,000 men over a 12 year period, those who had the lowest levels of beta-carotene had the highest mortality from lung cancer. The study also found that low levels of beta-carotene with low levels of vitamin A led to an increased risk of all types of cancers.

I encountered more studies about vitamin A or beta-carotene

(beta-carotene is a precursor to vitamin A) and cancer than any other nutrient in the medical literature. Most of these studies have shown a connection between taking vitamin A or beta-carotene and decreasing the risk of cancer. One study concluded that lower consumption of vitamin A and beta-carotene was a significant factor in contracting lung cancer; vitamin A was thought to inhibit tumor growth while beta-carotene appeared to inhibit tumor initiation. There have been other studies done with smokers that indicated the rate of lung cancer actually went up with beta-carotene. Although beta-carotene may help prevent cancer from forming, it may be of no value once the cancer has begun in a smoker.

According to one study, retinoids, which are vitamin A analogs, have actually reversed bronchial lesions caused by cigarette smoking. The foods that contain the most vitamin A are dark green, yellow and orange vegetables and fruits. Vitamin A is found in carrots, spinach, broccoli, apricots and peaches. There is a great deal of evidence that a diet high in these vegetables and fruits may prevent lung cancer. Many studies have found that the consumption of fruits and vegetables protects against cancers at many sites in the body, and the government now suggests that we eat at least five servings a day to help prevent tumors. The protective effect of fruits and vegetables is attributed to the various anticancer substances that they contain, including vitamins C and E, folic acid, carotenoids, flavonoids, isothiocyanates, phenols and fiber. My mother was delighted with the recent news from researchers at the University of Pennsylvania that chocolate is actually full of antioxidant compounds. The polyphenols in one piece of chocolate are equal to those in an entire day's worth of fruits and vegetables. Fruits and vegetables have other beneficial nutrients that chocloate does not have so it is not a good idea to substitute chocolate for fruits and vegetables. It is nice to know that we can eat chocolate and feel good about it. Another study showed a dose-response pattern: the more carotenoids eaten, the lower the risk of lung cancer. It appears that carotenoids stimulate the release of certain immune system cells into the body.

Beta-carotene levels in our blood may be reliable markers for letting us know if we're eating enough fruits and vegetables. One study of 25,000 volunteers from 1974 to 1975 found that serum beta-carotene levels showed a strong protective relationship to lung cancer. Consequently, low beta-carotene levels can precede an increase in lung cancer. In animal studies, injections of even low levels of beta-carotene has shown anticancer effects. Beta-carotene is also an antioxidant, which helps protect us from free radicals that cause DNA damage—the source of mutated cells that may become malignant. It has also been shown that exposure to the carcinogen, benzopyrene, in cigarette smoke can deplete the body of vitamin A.

Vitamin C

Vitamin C may have a stronger lung cancer benefit than beta-carotene. Thirty-three of 46 studies that evaluated vitamin C and cancer showed a significant protection. In 21 of 29 studies, eating fruit high in vitamin C was found to be cancer protective as well.

In a study that spanned two years, the plasma levels of vitamins A, C, and E were evaluated in nearly 3,000 men. Twelve years later it was found that 204 men had died from cancer. Overall, the authors of the study said plasma levels low in the antioxidant vitamins reflected an increased risk of cancer mortality. Vitamin C is a water-soluble antioxidant that reduces nitrites (often found in prepackaged lunch meats) and scavenges for free radicals. Vitamin E is a lipid-soluble antioxidant that prevents lipid peroxidation, which causes the release of harmful free radicals into the body.

One hundred "terminal" cancer patients were given vitamin

C supplementation of 10 g per day intravenously for 10 days and orally after that. It had already been determined that conventional treatment would be of no benefit. When those on vitamin C were compared to a similar control group who did not receive the supplement, the mean survival rate of those taking vitamin C was 4.2 times longer than those who did not receive it. Ninety percent of the vitamin C group died at one-third the rate of the controls and the other 10 percent had survival rates that were 90 percent greater than the control group. Some studies have indicated that vitamin C can also help with pain control in late-stage cancer. In a review article evaluating more than 90 different studies that looked at the role of vitamin C and cancer, most showed protective effects.

Vitamin E

One group of elderly patients taking 800 IU of vitamin E and another elderly group who took a multivitamin and mineral formulations as well as extra beta-carotene and vitamin E, showed significant improvement in their immune systems.

One study suggested that nonsmokers who eat foods high in beta-carotene and vitamins C and E have lowered their lung cancer risk by as much as 60 percent. Apparently smokers were unable to counter the effects of tobacco smoke with this diet and reap the favorable benefits. Another good reason to quit smoking now.

In yet another large study, a group of over 4,500 men who were cancer-free and between the ages of 20 and 69, were tracked over a period of 20 years. The authors of this study found a significant relationship between a decreased incidence of lung cancer and the intake of vitamins C, E, and the carotenoids. Again, smokers in the group did not benefit from higher doses of these vitamins.

Selenium

Selenium is considered an essential trace mineral or micronutrient. It is a powerful antioxidant with a central role in the protection of tissues from the damaging effects of oxygen free radicals. Although the role of selenium in cancer treatment is not clear, research suggests that selenium may play a role in reducing the risk of cancer by binding with glutathione peroxidase (GSH-Px) to combat destruction caused by free radicals and protecting cellular membranes. There appears to be a correlation between low levels of selenium in the diet and an increased risk of certain cancers. Miners in China, with low plasma and hair levels of selenium, were shown to have a high incidence of lung cancer. When selenium supplements were given, the minors developed increased protection against white blood cell DNA damage.

In a study of more than 1,000 subjects who had cancer, selenium or a placebo was given to each patient. The selenium supplementation correlated with a decrease in total cancer mortality, lung cancer mortality, total cancer incidence, and the incidence of colorectal and prostate cancers. The patients who received the selenium had an overall reduction of cancer of 41 percent and a 52 percent reduction in cancer mortality. In the United States, areas with the lowest soil selenium have a higher incidence of cancer. In another study in which patients received either 200 mcg of selenium or a placebo, there was a 50 percent lower cancer mortality rate in the selenium group. Lung and prostate cancer victims, in particular, had their mortality rates reduced.

Selenium may also help patients going through chemotherapy with the highly toxic drug cisplatin (Mother was on this drug during her treatment). When twenty patients were given 4,000 mcg of selenium 4 days before and 4 days after chemotherapy treatment, the white blood cells of those receiving the selenium were higher than those who did not receive it. Also nephrotoxicity (kidney toxicity) from the chemotherapy was significantly lower in the selenium group. Different types of cancers were involved in the study, including cancers of the lung, breast, stomach, colon, and esophagus.

Zinc

Zinc deficiency has been found in association with lung cancer as well as head and neck cancer, esophageal cancer and hepatocellular liver cancer. Zinc deficiency, which can have a detrimental effect on the immune system, can be associated with depressed numbers and response of T cells that are responsible for scavenging and destroying unwanted substances.

Magnesium

Magnesium is one of your body's most important coenzymes. It is essential for manufacturing hormones and the protein production process. It's also necessary for a healthy nervous and immune system. It has been shown that chemotherapy with Cisplatin can cause a magnesium deficiency. Since low magnesium levels account for neuromuscular irritability, weakness, confusion, seizures, cardiac arrhythmias, headaches, bronchial constriction and depression, it is no surprise that my mother had many of these symptoms during and after her chemotherapy treatments. This may very well be why she quickly perked up after each of her twice weekly magnesium injections.

Folic Acid

Folic acid works predominantly in the brain, nervous system, and is necessary in producing DNA and RNA. Brewers yeast, dark green leafy vegetables, wheat germ, oysters, salmon, and chicken are sources of folic acid. In at least one study performed on rats, folic acid was found to be cancer protective.

Diet and Nutrition

The influence of diet and nutrition on cancer has been studied a great deal. There are hundreds of studies in the medical literature that have examined the association of diet to cancers in general, and to lung cancer specifically. Almost every study has shown a positive correlation between eating fruits and vegetables and having a lower risk of cancer. Animals who are fed fruits and vegetables before and after being exposed to carcinogens are less likely to develop cancer. It seems cruciferous vegetables, such as broccoli, Brussels sprouts, cabbage, cauliflower, bok choy, kale, mustard greens, rutabaga, turnips and turnip greens have a chemical agent that helps break down carcinogens. Onions, garlic, leeks and chives appear to contain another chemical that helps the body remove cancer-causing agents.

One study indicated that there was a strong correlation between eating dark green and yellow vegetables and cancer risk: more vegetables, less risk. By making vegetables into a cold soup called gazpacho, my mother could swallow the vegetables more easily. Many studies evaluating groups of over 200 people found a relationship between eating fruits and vegetables and contracting a variety of different cancers—128 of 156 studies found this protective effect from eating fruits and vegetables. In 24 of 25 studies of lung cancer and diet, fruit and vegetable consumption was found to significantly lower lung cancer risk. Researchers believe the protection comes from several different mechanisms: detoxification, interfering with the formation of nitrosamines, diluting and binding of carcinogenic substances in the gastrointestinal tract, modifying hormones, antioxidant effect and providing substrates for anticancer substances. I recommend eating only organic fruits and vegetables.

Other foods associated with possible protection from cancer are those containing lignans and isoflavonoids and phytoestrogens. Where these are found in high levels in the plasma, there is also found a low incidence of cancer. These compounds are best found in soybean products, whole grains, seeds and berries.

Soy

Soybeans and soybean products are a staple of the Japanese diet, and for good reason. Scientific research has identified healing agents in soybeans, called glycosides. Glycosides contain substances that protect the cell from oxidation from the low density lipoproteins found in "bad" cholesterol. Rather than rely on foods high in saturated fats for protein that can damage tissues (hamburger, pork, dairy, chicken, and pork), we should balance our diet and use high-protein soy products often.

Garlic

Garlic, perhaps one of the best-known folk medicines, is a potent antioxidant just like vitamins A, C, and E and has been shown to reduce lung cancer in mice. Studies have shown that garlic boosts the body's immune system, thins the blood, and reduces cholesterol.

Watercress

Watercress was given to eleven smokers who ate it at three meals per day. Chewing watercress was found to release a chemical which has been shown to prevent lung cancer in rats who were given nicotine carcinogens. It appeared that the chemical in the watercress at least partially blocked the activity of the tobacco-specific lung carcinogens.

Essential Fatty Acids

The importance of essential fatty acids should not be over-looked when it comes to cancer either. Groups of patients with tumors were evaluated for the benefits of the omega-3 fatty acids. In each group there were 15 malnourished and 15 well-nourished individuals. The group supplemented with fish oil of 18g/day and 200mg of vitamin E did better than the group receiving the placebo. Patients in the well-nourished group had an edge that resulted in a higher overall survival rate. Those who received the fish oil in the malnourished group had a better survival rate as well. Fish oil may play a role in interfering with cell proliferation connected with tumor growth. You can get adequate amounts of omega-3 by eating salmon or flaxseed.

Weight Loss

Weight loss has been associated with a significantly lower rate of surviving cancer. It's difficult to keep weight on when suffering the side effects of chemotherapy—nausea, vomiting, and loss of appetite. Mother did lose some weight, but not a lot since we were on top of the nutrition situation from the beginning on a daily basis during treatment. There is evidence that daily nutritional repletion enriches the immune system and consequently improves tumor reduction from chemotherapy. While loss of too much weight is a poor prognosticator in cancer, obesity may increase the progression of a malignant disease.

Cholesterol: It's Not What You Think

The relation of serum cholesterol to the development of cancer remains unclear. Surprisingly, low levels of cholesterol are associated with increased cancer risk. In one study of more than 1200 adult men who were tracked for an average of 10 years, the men with the lowest cholesterol levels had nearly double the cancer incidence and mortality. While too much fat is associated with cancer increase, too low cholesterol levels are as well. When more than 6,000 French men, ages 43 to 52, were studied for a correlation between cholesterol and cancer, the group having the highest decline in cholesterol had the highest risk for most cancers. It should be noted that even though obesity is a factor for increased cancer risk, all obese people do not have high cholesterol. There's also another possibility here. Although low cholesterol seems to increase the risk of cancer, it may be that preclinical cancer in some way lowers serum cholesterol—which changes the spin on the entire matter.

Trans-Fatty Acids

Many studies suggest we should avoid hydrogenated or partially hydrogenated vegetable oils. I agree. Hydrogenated oils contain harmful trans-fatty acids (TFAs) which should be eliminated from your diet as much as possible. Most TFAs are produced in a chemical process called hydrogenation or partial hydrogenation, used to make liquid oils solid or semisolid at room temperature, such as margarine and vegetable shortening. These oils go into most mass-produced baked goods.

Clinical studies have shown that TFAs can raise total blood cholesterol levels just as saturated fats (from meat and dairy products) do. TFAs also raise LDL ("bad") cholesterol and lower HDL ("good") cholesterol. Although we know that the body uses natural fatty acids to construct cell membranes and hormones, we don't know how it handles TFAs. There is reason to believe these fats cause aberrations of cell structure, thus promoting cancer. Figuring out which foods contain TFAs isn't easy, since hydrogenated oils are not listed on the packaging.

When you look at a content label, the amount of fat is listed as the number of grams of fat in the product. The fat grams are broken down into saturated, monounsaturated or polyunsaturated. These numbers don't always add up to the total number of fat grams. While the number of hydrogenated fat grams are not listed in the breakdown, they are included in the total. If, for example, the total number of grams of fat is 5 and there are 2 grams of saturated, 1 gram of polyunsaturated and 1 gram of monounsaturated, there is still one gram of fat unaccounted for in the total. That one gram is the hydrogenated fat. If the total of the different fats is equal to the total listed then there are no hydrogenated fats in the product. Check the labels of any processed foods you buy and avoid those containing hydrogenated or partially hydrogenated oils of any kind.

The safest fats are monounsaturated, such as olive oil, canola oil (organic, expeller-pressed variety sold in health food stores), as well as the omega-3 fatty acids found in fish. These oils also act as anti-inflammatory agents and are important natural treatments for autoimmune disorders and arthritis.

More Bad Foods

In another study it was found that the following foods are related to an increase in lung cancer: bacon, sausage, lunch meat, whole milk, ice cream, eggs, fruit pies, custard and cream pies. Luncheon meats, sausage and bacon contain nitrates and some studies show a positive correlation between nitrates and cancer. The other foods, ice cream and pies are often high in trans-fatty acids and saturated fats and cholesterol. This study also found that the highest correlation between food and lung cancer was in men who were smokers.

Sugar

According to several studies, high sugar intake may increase the risk factor for cancer by having an adverse affect on the immune system. If Mother thought eating more vegetables was difficult, there was no question that avoiding sugar was the toughest of all. Although my mother loves sugar, I was able to get her to cut way back. She was satisfied as long as she could have just a small piece of chocolate candy after dinner. After all, some might say, if you can't have chocolate, is there any reason to live? Another way to satisfy your sweet tooth is with fruit.

Tea

In Japan, a lower incidence of lung cancer is thought to be associated with the high intake of tea. John H. Weisburger, Ph.D., who is involved in tea research at The American Health Foundation, recommends drinking four to five cups of tea daily. Drinking green tea, in particular, has been shown to inhibit lung tumor induction by 50 percent in mice. Apparently, tea has very good antioxidant potential. Other studies support that drinking green tea helps decrease the incidence of such cancers as stomach, esophagus, liver and lung cancer. One study found that "Daily tea consumption significantly reduced the risk of squamous cell cancer in males and females." Drinking 4 or more cups of tea per day (green tea is preferred) had the same benefit as eating 2 of the 5 recommended servings of vegetables and fruits.

Panax Ginseng

Ginseng is an ancient herb widely known for improving stamina and helping the body cope with stress. Germanium, one of the elements found in ginseng, is a chelator—meaning it can draw out heavy metals, such as mercury, lead, or cadmium from the body. According to a study given at the Third International Symposium on Ginseng in Korea, ginseng also has the apparent ability to protect bone marrow against radioactivity. Mice pre-treated with ginseng survived intense x-ray radiation at a rate exceeding 82 percent over the control group. In human studies done in Korea, Panax ginseng (meaning the Chinese variety) consumption correlated with a lower incidence of cancer. Along with its anticarcinogenic effects, Panax ginseng has a low toxicity according to this study and should be a safe food in cancer prevention.

Alcohol and Drug Abuse

There are many studies that indicate a relationship between alcohol intake and lung cancer. My mother is not a heavy drinker, having an occasional drink with dinner. Still, she was advised to avoid alcohol completely.

One study found beer consumption to be a predictor of lung cancer risk. It's best to limit consumption of all alcohol, if you drink at all. Alcoholic beverages, along with cigarette smoking and use of snuff and chewing tobacco, cause cancers of the oral cavity, esophagus, and larynx. The use of both alcohol and to-bacco produces a synergistic effect and a cancer risk greater than the sum of their individual effects.

From the American Cancer Society comes this advice:

Living with cancer and undergoing cancer treatment does not usually lead people to misuse drugs or alcoholic bever-ages. But some people have drug or alcohol problems before they learn about their cancer. If you drink excessively or use drugs, it is very important that you deal with these problems before and during cancer treatment. Drinking and drug abuse can make your cancer care less effective or more diffi-cult for you. For example:

- If you need surgery, drugs or alcohol in your body can create problems with the medicine needed to put you to sleep (anesthesia).
- If you are being treated with cancer drugs (chemother-apy), you may get sores in your mouth, and alcohol will make them worse.
- If you need radiation treatment or chemotherapy, you will need to eat well to stay strong. Drinking or taking drugs can interfere with good eating habits and a quick recovery.
- Drug and alcohol abuse will keep you from coping well with cancer and its stresses and emotional demands.

Coping with cancer can be hard. Drinking and drugs will not help you cope. Their use may also hinder your cancer treat-ment.

Radon

There are other environmental factors influencing lung can-cer and one of them is radon.

Radon is a radioactive gas released from the decay of ura-nium in rocks and soil. It is an invisible, odorless, and tasteless gas that seeps up through the ground and diffuses into the air. In a few areas, depending on local geology, radon dissolves at high concentrations in groundwater where it can then be released into the air when this water is used. Out of doors, radon gas ex-ists at harmless levels. However, in areas without adequate ventilation, such as underground mines, radon can accumulate to levels that substantially increase the risk of lung cancer.

Radon quickly decays, emitting tiny radioactive particles. When inhaled, these radioactive particles can damage the cells lining the lung. Long-term exposure to radon can lead to lung cancer, the only cancer proven to be associated with inhaling radon. Everyone breathes in radon every day, but mostly at very low levels resulting in little adverse effect. However, people who inhale high levels of radon gas may be at an increased risk for developing lung cancer.

Radon enters homes through cracks and holes in the foundation, and can even be released from running water—though radon from water makes a substantial contribution to total indoor radon levels in only a few areas of the country. Radon levels measure the highest in homes that are well insulated, tightly sealed, and/or built on uranium-rich soil. Because of their closeness to the ground, basement and first floors typically have the highest radon levels.

In 1992, a government assessment of exposure to radon concluded that 13,600 lung cancer deaths per year could be as a result of radon exposure. Today, radon-associated lung cancers per year may be as high as 36,000. Although the association between radon exposure and smoking is not well understood, exposure to the combination of radon gas and cigarette smoke creates a greater risk for lung cancer than either alone. The majority of radon-related cancer deaths occur among smokers.

There is a simple test available to determine if you have high levels of radon in your home. My parents checked their home and found no radon present.

Exercise and Cancer

When cancer patients receiving chemotherapy were also put on an exercise program, they had a decisive advantage over those who didn't exercise. They had fewer problems with low white blood cell and platelet counts, less severe diarrhea, less severe pain and shorter hospital stays.

Tests and Cancer Detection

In addition to familiar MRI, CT, and bone scans

New: *Ultra fast CT Scan*

Test that shows if there is cancer anywhere in the body
This test shows all the organs, blood vessels and tissues inside the body between the waist and the shoulders and can detect very small cancers, particularly in the lungs. After the test was performed on my mother, 8 years after having cancer, we were shown a computer-generated view of how everything in the upper part of her body looked. As the doctor took us through Mother's body on the computer screen, we could see for ourselves that there were no visible signs of cancer. How reassuring!

The Enemy Within

"Smoking kills more people every year than alcohol, cocaine, crack, heroin, homicide, suicide, car accidents, fire and AIDS combined. The take home message is don't ever start smoking."
—Deepak Chopra

According to the American Cancer Society, "This year about 563,100 Americans are expected to die of cancer, more than 1500 people a day. Cancer is the second leading cause of death in the U.S., exceeded only by heart disease. In the U.S., 1 of 4 deaths is from cancer. Nearly five million lives have been lost to cancer since 1990."

In simple terms, cancer is a disease marked by the uncontrolled growth of abnormal or mutated cells. The abnormal cells may no longer do the work of normal cells, and they crowd out and destroy healthy tissue. The body's own cells have mutated and are on a singular self-destruct mission. Although lung cancer takes many years to develop, subtle changes in the lung can begin almost immediately upon exposure to carcinogens (cancer-causing substances). Soon after exposure begins, microscopic examination of the tissue lining the bronchi (the main breathing tubes) will reveal a few unusual cells. With continued exposure, more abnormal cells appear. These cells may be on their way to becoming cancerous and forming a tumor.

Although warnings about cigarette smoking are ubiquitous in modern society, the toll of lung cancer continues to rise, taking some one million lives around the world each year. Despite these grim statistics, there is room for optimism because lung cancer is also among the most preventable of all cancers. The 1964 landmark *Smoking and Health Report* of the Advisory Committee to the Surgeon General clearly linked tobacco use as the greatest risk factor in contracting lung cancer. Subsequent studies have shown that as many as 9 out of 10 cases of lung cancer are caused by smoking. The most effective way to lower your risk is never to smoke, or if you do, to stop now.

There are two common types of lung cancer—small cell and nonsmall cell. Both are associated with smoking. Small cell cancer, also known as oat cell cancer for its microscopic resemblance to the grain, occurs almost exclusively in smokers. Accounting for about 20 percent of the lung cancers in the United States, small cell cancer is a fast-growing tumor that quickly spreads to other organs. This is the cell type of Mimi's cancer. At the time of diagnosis, this type of cancer has already spread (metastasized) in nearly 70 percent of its victims. Without treatment, the tumor will lead to death within several months. Nonsmall cell lung cancer is more common than the small cell type. It appears in three types: squamous cell carcinoma (the most common type of lung cancer in men), adenocarcinoma (the most common lung cancer in women and people who have never smoked (Cele contracted this type), and large cell carcinoma (originating at the periphery of the lungs).

Because the lungs are abundantly supplied by blood and lymph from the lymphatic drainage system, lung cancer spreads more easily to other parts of the body than do many other cancers. The lymphatic system includes tissues and organs that produce, store, and carry cells that fight infection and disease. This system includes the bone marrow, spleen, thymus, and lymph nodes.

Is Your Biology Your Destiny?

Whether you are male or female, you are at increased risk if there is cancer in your family. Your risk is greater still if there is cancer on both sides of your family. Being at risk, however, doesn't mean you will contract the disease; it does mean you need to be alert and proactive about prevention. I am.

The genetic component of lung cancer is never completely out of my awareness. Although cancer often runs in families, a predisposition to the disease may be inherited, not the cancer itself. Additionally, some diseases that seem to run in families can often be traced to shared environmental exposures rather than any inherited genetic susceptibility. The overwhelming majority of cancers that befall us stem from random mutations that develop in body cells during one's lifetime. These mutations occur either as a mistake when cells are going through cell division, or in response to injuries from environmental insults such as radiation or chemicals.

My grandmother on my mother's side and my father's brother died from lung cancer. And then my mother had it, too. I accept the causal relationship between tobacco smoking and lung cancer. With two generations of lung cancer on both sides of my immediate family tree, I don't want to add any further risk toward developing lung cancer myself. By avoiding tobacco fumes, including secondhand smoke, I maintain a strong set of lungs and diffuse the predisposition factor. I don't like being around tobacco smoke. It makes me sick and this reaction helps keep me healthy.

Thanks to my mother, I don't have a role model for dying. I have a role model for living. I take most of the vitamins and minerals I had recommended that Cele take during her treatment. If these nutrients bolstered Mother's recovery from a "lost cause," I'm confident they'll also help prevent cancer from ever finding a place in my body.

Writing this book has reenergized my dominant proactive gene, a genetic "predisposition" based on attitude, not genealogy. We can choose our reality. Why wait until something terrible happens to start taking care of yourself. This isn't just rosy thinking on my part. Most cancers are preventable by making lifestyle changes, which often seem difficult to accomplish. But when you look at the alternative, "difficult" becomes exceedingly doable and downright necessary for enjoying life. Of course, quitting smoking and avoiding sidestream smoke tops the list in preventing lung cancer. Preempt the scare. You don't want to hear your doctor tell you that you've got lung cancer. Find out what to do to stay healthy and do it.

Another World

"When some folks agree with my opinions I begin to suspect I'm wrong." —Kin Hubbard

Once upon a time doctors in the U.S. used to make house calls. Then, the world changed. Since my mother had fallen ill with lung cancer 10 years ago, the world has become a different place once again. While I had to hunt for existing complementary modalities, such treatments have slowly gained wider acceptance among the public and with doctors. In addition, new treatments have surfaced into the mainstream as well.

For resourceful individuals of today, there is a wealth of information available in books, magazines, workshops, survivor groups, and on Web sites. Anyone with Internet access (free at many public libraries) can log on to the World Wide Web and search for the most up-to-date cancer treatment data available anywhere in the world—from large research centers to individual physicians. The Web is an unprecedented and invaluable resource for doing research on just about any subject, including the vast domain of health care and disease prevention.

Patients are finding our health care system increasingly disappointing. Although it seems logical that the health industry would look into alternative protocols, overcoming the inertia of the existing power structure and corporate self interest will only happen when the public has had enough. These days, more and more patients are asking questions that their doctors are not trained to answer. Left to their own devices, people in need must get information from wherever they can. Whether the information is sound is another issue. Making sure your source is trustworthy is not always black and white, especially when you're dying.

Instead of drugs and mainstream "wisdom," millions of Americans have been turning to natural supplements and alternative therapies. Our health care system isn't progressive. For example, although much data on botanical medicine exists in support of its therapeutic value and safety, most doctors in the States haven't got a clue. When it comes to research in this area, Japan, Germany, France and Russia have left the American medical establishment in the Dark Ages.

What good is a cornucopia of information if you can't use any of it to get well? Many cancer patients cannot discuss alternative measures with their own doctors. They can't even coordinate complementary with traditional treatments because their conventional-minded oncologists are negative about unconventional protocols. Finding the right doctor is as rare as finding a cure—especially with cancer. Keep in mind that only minor advances in fighting cancer with conventional means have been made in the past 50 years. On the upside, there have been substantial improvements in early detection and diagnosis, which have improved the statistical mainstream cure rate—alive five years after the diagnosis.

Oncologists know going in that you're coming to them with the hope that they have a cure. Oncologists know that lung cancer patients have little chance for a cure. They know what the success rate of their treatment has been in the past. In this book, you've read about my frustration at finding help from conventional medicine for my grandmother, and then years later for my mother. So, the question is simple: Is your physician willing to increase your life expectancy by expanding his horizons? Sure, it takes more energy and a time commitment to investigate new ways of healing. Cures are not discovered by the timid. If you know your chances are slim to none and your doctor insists on following narrow party line parameters and low success rates, then it's all up to you—the very same advice I gave my mother. There is no conclusive agreement concerning the nature of cancer as a disease. Is it the disease manifesting itself as a localized tumor, or is it symptomatic of a body-wide immune malfunction we don't yet comprehend? Since we don't have an answer to the cancer puzzle or a definitive cure, patients must investigate and initiate all potentially lifesaving treatments. You must take charge as if your life depends upon it.

It would be measurably more productive if a patient could have unfettered assistance with both conventional and alternative treatments. If oncologists would team up with doctors like myself, their patients would receive the nutritional support and osteopathic benefits they need while undergoing chemotherapy or radiation. Such a collaboration would in no way undermine conventional treatment.

After having read this book, you may have concluded that I'm in the eclectic camp and hold no partisan allegiances. I voted my conscience and swam against the mainstream to help save my mother's life. In my practice, patients on the mend are my constituency. Since I can only get votes of confidence from living souls, I'm committed to reaping the best of both conventional and alternative treatments without placing politically divisive labels on either. Instead of allowing myself to get polarized in a black-and-white reality during my mother's bout with cancer, I took the middle path, which should not be confused with sitting on the fence, average, or mediocre. The middle path is that fine line of harmonious balance where I found the strength and the tools to save Cele. If we're on the right path, we will stumble upon the same universal truths and find out for ourselves.

Although the chemotherapy and radiation were brutal on Mother, I believe their controlled violence knocked her cancer into a stupor and were absolutely necessary. The noninvasive natural remedies helped her survive these mainstream treatments by rebuilding her immune system, which ultimately eliminated the cancer completely. There have been individuals who questioned both sides of my mother's protocol. Conventional thinkers discounted the alternative methods, while alternative proponents questioned why I would put my mother through chemotherapy and radiation with all their side effects. There is no doubt in my mind that both were necessary. We will never know which treatments could have been left out. Could I have saved my mother from experiencing the damage from chemotherapy and radiation? I was not going to risk her life on it. I was also not going to wait to see if the conventional treatments would cure her before starting the alternative ones. This plan may be why so many alternative techniques fail. When the conventional oncologist has done all he can, he then may tell the patient, "Try anything now." This may be "too little too late." How much better it would be if the two camps would work together as we did with my mother's case. It would be exciting to see what results might come of it.

Smoking: Puff, the Not-So-Magic Dragon

"I am disturbed when I see a cigarette between the lips or fingers of some important person upon whose intelligence and judgment the welfare of the world in part depends." —Linus Pauling

As the American Lung Association says: "When you can't breathe, nothing else matters." I am emphatic with patients who come to my office. My rule is simple: Smoking is not an option! Adult smokers must agree to quit or I will not treat them. I will, however, help them quit—which must be dealt with on a case-by-case basis.

If a child is my patient and the parents smoke, they must agree to cease smoking in the house, in the car—anywhere in the child's environment, even if the child isn't there at the time. Harmful chemicals linger and permeate the furniture, fabrics, clothing, walls, and the confined interior of an automobile or a room.

A cigarette is basically a nicotine delivery device. Each pack of cigarettes has been clearly labeled since 1966 with a warning that the smokes you're about to light up will most likely kill you—a serious prediction that's routinely ignored. Over 90 percent of lung cancers are caused by cigarette smoking. Not only is there empirical proof that smoking causes lung cancer, it has been shown, according to former U.S. Surgeon General C. Everett Koop, that nicotine is as addictive as heroin and cocaine. If there's any doubt, try taking the last pack away from a hardened smoker, and do so at your own risk. Some years back, a shocking public service antismoking ad was used effectively. The simple ad featured a photograph of a throat cancer victim smoking a cigarette through a tracheotomy—a hole cut in his throat so he could breathe. Addiction? You be the judge.

My dear grandmother died from lung cancer. Although she never smoked in her life, Mimi lived with my aunt Marie and uncle Jack—both smoked heavily for years prior to the 1964 Surgeon General's report. Prior to the government's announcement on the proven dangers of smoking, it was nearly impossible to avoid tobacco smoke in most public areas.

As a young child, I remember sitting in movie theaters while people puffed away on their cigarettes and the smoke drifted thick through the brightly focused beam of the film projector. It's hard to believe today, but cigarette smoke used to be everywhere. Although my aunt and uncle both quit smoking as soon as the Surgeon General's report was released, the damage of secondhand smoke had already been done to Mimi's more susceptible lungs.

You may have heard some person, usually a smoker, saying something to this effect: "Oh heck, my Grandpa Ed smoked two packs . . . the old unfiltered kind . . . a day and he lived to be ninety-three years old." While such a statement may be a fact, science doesn't know why some people get cancer and others don't—and Grandpa Ed may have lived to be an even riper age without smoking. Although we don't yet have the answer about the fundamental cause of cancer, we do have the apt question of prevention to consider. Do you want to smoke and gamble with your life knowing that cigarettes dramatically increase your chances of developing lung cancer, other cancers, or other life-threatening illnesses?

The scenario repeated itself with my mother. My father smoked heavily and my mother called herself a "social" smoker who'd hold a burning cigarette between her fingers when she was in the company of her smoking cronies. She didn't inhale. She didn't have to. All she had to do was breathe. By some estimates, breathing in carcinogenic secondhand, or sidestream smoke, is the equivalent of smoking four to twenty cigarettes a day. Following in Mimi's footsteps, "Nonsmoker" Cele eventually developed lung cancer. Fortunately for my father, he was like my aunt and uncle—the cancer resistant Grandpa Ed type.

When I was a teenager in the early '60s, I began smoking to impress a boy I had just met. I didn't realize at the time that my decision was more than foolish; it was dangerous. I never really liked smoking and still remember my "first puff." I had the usual automatic reflex experience. I nearly choked to death. The body doesn't need a federal committee, a clinical trial, a double blind study, or a second opinion to confirm that it's being poisoned. My body's innate intelligence was telling me to stop. But, did I listen?

Like so many other high school kids, I persevered and soon joined the ranks of the very much addicted. Of course, the general public was not yet aware of the dangers of smoking—which was still a tobacco industry secret back then. I smoked all the time and did so for five compulsive years until the 1964 Surgeon General report shocked me and my smoking family into waking up. Smoking was a nasty habit that was socially acceptable just about everywhere. When I was in college, smokers were lighting up in class without restriction. Not everyone bent under peer pressure. My brother, Steve, for example, who was on the high school swimming team, never did smoke and he hated to be around it. His coach understood the debilitating effects smoking had on lungs and athletic performance. Sports and cigarettes didn't mix. If the coach wanted to have a winning swim team, he wasn't going to let his team's chances for success go up in smoke.

Nailing Your Own Coffin: Is There Really Any Doubt?

Smoking "coffin nails" is the number one cause of lung cancer. Cigarette smoke contains more than 4,000 different chemicals. Over 50 compounds in cigarette smoke were identified as carcinogens, and six were blamed for reproductive or developmental problems. Children are especially susceptible to smoke-related respiratory illnesses like asthma.

Paralleling the steady rise in cigarette smoking in this century, lung cancer has become the most common cancer-related cause of death among men and women. If you smoke, you are much more likely to develop lung cancer; men who smoke are estimated to be 22 times more likely to develop the disease, while women who smoke are estimated to be 12 times more likely.

The more you smoke and the longer you smoke, the greater your risk of lung cancer. If you stop smoking, the risk of cancer decreases steadily each year as abnormal cells are replaced by normal cells. In 10 years, the risk decreases to a level that is 30 to 50 percent of the risk for people who continue to smoke. In addition, quitting smoking dramatically reduces the risk of developing other smoking-related diseases, such as heart disease and stroke, and significantly reduces the risk of emphysema and chronic bronchitis.

It has been estimated that there were over 170,000 new cases of lung cancer in the U.S. in 1998 alone. Although the rate of lung cancer cases appears to be declining among white men in the U.S., it continues to increase among black men and among both white and black women. Lung cancer incidence has increased fivefold in women over the past 50 years, correlating proportionately with an increase in smoking among more "liberated" women. Looking at mortality statistics alone, nearly one of every 5 deaths in the U.S. is attributed to tobacco.

Abundant evidence has established the causal relationship between the use of tobacco and cancer, cardiovascular disease, chronic obstructive lung disease, peripheral vascular disease, stroke, and a variety of serious pediatric maladies in children exposed to secondhand smoke. Over 160,000 Americans died due to lung cancer in 1998. Probably one-fifth of all cancer deaths in the United States are due to lung tumors directly caused by smoking and tobacco-related diseases and conditions, which kills 430,000 people per year—the population of a fairly large city. The American Cancer Society says that more than 1.2 million Americans will be diagnosed with cancer and that 563,000 of them will die of the disease in 1999—most of them smokers.

While deaths associated with illegal drugs account for 20,000 deaths per year, there are 50 million legal nicotine addicts in America and another fifty million are ex-smokers. Approximately one-third of our population is at high risk for not only lung cancer but for multiple other tobacco-related diseases, including cancers of the mouth, tongue, throat, larynx, esophagus, pancreas, bladder and kidney, plus coronary artery disease, peripheral artery disease, gangrene of the legs and stroke. Of those who now smoke, 82 percent were addicted as children and all were addicted at a time when the tobacco industry emphatically assured the public that their legally supported and commercially promoted products were not harmful to health, nor was nicotine addictive. In 1994, top executives of the largest tobacco manufacturers in the U.S. stood before a congressional committee and testified under oath that tobacco does not kill, nicotine is not addictive, and denied that they were marketing to kids.

Nonsmokers exposed to smoke are also at an increased risk for lung cancer. A nonsmoker married to a smoker has a 30 percent greater risk of developing lung cancer than the spouse of a nonsmoker. Environmental tobacco smoke (ETS), also known as secondhand smoke, comes from two places: smoke breathed out by the person who smokes, and smoke from the end of a burning cigarette. ETS causes or exacerbates a wide range of adverse health effects, including cancer, respiratory infections, and asthma.

The American Lung Association Fact Sheet on Environmental Tobacco Smoke (ETS) shows that

- ETS contains over 4,000 chemicals; 200 are poisons; 43 cause cancer. ETS has been classified by the Environmental Protection Agency (EPA) as a known cause of cancer in humans (Group A carcinogen).
- ETS causes lung cancer and other health problems. The EPA estimates that ETS causes approximately 3,000 lung cancer deaths and 37,000 heart disease deaths in nonsmokers each year.
- ETS is especially harmful to young children. The EPA estimates that ETS is responsible for between 150,000 and 300,000 lower respiratory tract infections in infants and children under 18 months of age annually, resulting in between 7,500 and 15,000 hospitalizations each year.
- ETS is harmful to children with asthma. The EPA estimates that for between 200,000 and one million asthmatic children, exposure to ETS worsens their condition.
- ETS can make healthy children less than 18 months of age sick; it can cause pneumonia, ear infections, bronchitis, coughing, wheezing and increased mucus production. According to the EPA, ETS can lead to the buildup of fluid in the middle ear, the most common cause of hospitalization of children for an operation.

In the U.S., secondhand smoke is now recognized as a significant health threat. Looking at passive smoking and its relationship to lung cancer, one study found approximately 17 percent of lung cancers in nonsmokers related to passive smoke exposure in childhood. Exposure to smoke for 25 years or more during childhood doubled the risk of lung cancer.

The EPA recently released the most damaging report ever on secondhand smoke. The agency's first study on the subject in 1993 found that secondhand smoke caused 3,000 cases of lung cancer annually, but its new report adds to the toll with up to 62,000 heart disease deaths, 2,700 deaths from sudden-infant-death syndrome, and 2,600 new cases of asthma. The report also implicates secondhand smoke as a risk factor in spontaneous abortions and cervical cancer. The tobacco industry dismissed these new findings and is suing the EPA. Cigarette manufacturers have long maintained that they have refrained from manipulating the nicotine levels in cigarettes. The FDA, referring to tobacco industry documents going back 20 years recommending nicotine manipulation, contends that manufacturers have been adding ammonia specifically to boost the amount of addictive nicotine absorbed by smokers.

Cigarettes on Celluloid

The tobacco industry has been successfully dumping huge sums of money for years into advertising and public relations campaigns aimed at hooking young people on smoking. As the children of the 1980s reached adolescence, teen tobacco use rose dramatically—32 percent from 1991 to 1998. After about 100 cigarettes, the typical teen becomes addicted and continues smoking for 16 to 20 years. Ninety percent of new smokers are children and teenagers. The new smokers replace the smoker who quit or died prematurely, most likely from a smoking-related disease. As the number of smokers increase, the number of deaths from lung cancer increases. When I go about my daily business, it's alarming to see so many teenage boys and girls smoking, feeling they are being grown up and cool—not unlike myself when I was in high school. But back then we didn't know the horrible truth about smoking.

In addition to its own misinformation efforts on behalf of the joys of smoking, the tobacco industry has bought off Hollywood. I'm convinced of it. Specific brands of soft drinks, candies, coffee, fast foods, alcohol, beer, and cigarettes don't appear in films by accident. According to a *Minneapolis Star and Tribune* article, "Smoking Out Payoffs For Placing Tobacco Product In Movies" by Nancy Marsden, "Congress has long been aware that the Philip Morris Companies paid to 'place' Marlboro cigarettes and signage in the first and second *Superman* movies."

On December 4, 1997, the Commerce Committee of the United States House of Representatives subpoenaed over 800 tobacco industry documents in the matter of *State of Minnesota v. Philip Morris, Inc.* Minnesota wants to recover health care and other costs resulting from the use of tobacco products. In a poetic plot twist, access to the evidence subpoenaed in the Minnesota lawsuit against the tobacco companies also raised new concerns about Hollywood's tobacco connection. Three pages of a memo unearthed by the Minnesota Attorney General's office details the contractual relationship between Philip Morris and the *Superman II* producers to market Marlboro cigarettes to children in consideration for "twenty thousand pounds sterling."

In 1988, Philip Morris forked over $350,000 to feature Lark cigarettes in the James Bond film, *License to Kill.* Marsden writes that subpoenaed documents from Philip Morris state that "product was supplied" for more than 190 movies during the decade from 1978 to1988. In addition, Marsden adds, "The shocking, 14-page list of titles peaks in '87 and '88, when the company supplied tobacco for 54 films, including youth fare like

The Dream Team, Crocodile Dundee, Robocop, Die Hard, and *Who Framed Roger Rabbit?* Fifty films, such as *The Muppet Movie, Grease* and *Jaws II,* were rated PG or G." According to Philip Morris, these placements were "donations" and no record of payments has been uncovered. Such evidence may have been destroyed, or the deal made orally. But more to the point, as Marsden's article brings out, if such advertising was free, why did the company pay $350,000 the same year for a prominent product role in *License to Kill?*

Either way, Hollywood's standard disclaimer—that films don't influence behavior is ridiculous. Television is on the same wavelength. Seeing famous actors taking a big sexy, tough, debonair, relaxing, name-your-adjective drag on the silver screen is an indelible image and influence on impressionable minds, especially the young. If movies could not recruit smokers, tobacco executives would not bother. Why pay the money for embedded advertising or take any potential risks of negative press? In her article, Marsden notes that "The memos leaked from Brown & Williamson suggesting that, back in the early 1980s, A-list movie stars accepted gifts for smoking in movies. Luxury cars, jewelry and cash payments of up to $300,000 were allegedly channeled through a now defunct product placement agency, at a cost of $950,000."

The power of product placement follows one god—the bottom line. When Tom Cruise donned a pair of Ray-Ban sunglasses in *Risky Business,* the company enjoyed a 55 percent gain in sales. Reese's Pieces candy sales sweetened upward by 65 percent after an appearance in *E.T.* When the "Fonz" got a library card in the TV sitcom *Happy Days,* applications for library cards across the country increased. More recently, whether secret payoffs may have been made to the makers of such recent, smoking-intensive movies as *Independence Day, Titanic,* and *My Best Friend's Wedding* remains a matter of intelligent speculation. I think you get the picture.

Throughout this book I've extolled the benefits of positive suggestion through hypnosis and guided imagery. These very same techniques can be used for nefarious purposes as well. The movie industry churns out dreams on film that have a mass hypnosis impact of tremendous power over most of us, especially children and young adults who are trying to establish their individuality—often attempting to do so by some twisted logic that involves conforming to peer behavior.

Today, since smoking is finally banned in most communal spaces, this generation of children doesn't view it as normal to see people smoking in public. I am disappointed in the movie industry and hope to see studio executives act responsibly in the future when it comes to the public interest. Our health should not be for sale.

Tobacco Road

The volume of information about the tobacco industry that's available to the average citizen today is staggering. To read and absorb the enormous amount of material is a daunting task. Such content has become possible because of the Web and instant access to many watchdog group sites, and even the tobacco companies themselves who have been ordered by the courts to disclose internal documents. There is only one central issue that concerns me. Cigarette smoking is addictive and deadly. It's a fact and the proof is readily available.

In the past several years, the media has been routinely reporting on the ongoing million and billion dollar lawsuits being waged against our domestic tobacco cartel. The tobacco industry knows that if they don't hook kids on nicotine early, the chances are they won't become habitual smokers as they mature into adults. Nothing personal. Destroying health and killing people is called business as usual. Whatever happened to making decisions based on the public good? As of this writing, the major party presidential candidates are scrambling to appear smoke-free, yet have hired campaign aides with strong links to tobacco. I question the ethics of aides who run to the highest bidder and the candidates who knowingly employ them. For years, tobacco has been one of the most "generous" of political donors. Trying to sit on the fence while attempting to wean themselves from the far-reaching influence of tobacco's money, these "bought" politicians will be forced to eventually enact legislation in the public interest, or look for new work.

Recently, internal "privileged" and incriminating memos from various tobacco firms show that they have known for years about cigarettes' harmful effects and the addictive nature of nicotine. In fact, the basis for many of the lawsuits brought against the tobacco industry is that they "willfully" advertised and sold addictive products known to cause injury.

Tobacco is a curious commodity. In 1776, little, if anything, was known of the direct health hazards of smoking. Since income generated from tobacco sales played such a decisive role in financing the Revolutionary War, the tobacco industry has prospered big time and pretty much unregulated for some 200 years with the blessings of the United States Congress. The "friendly" cash crop that helped cultivate the creation of this nation has now become an enemy of the people. Caught in a threshing machine of historical precedent, corporate conspiracies to withhold information about the addictive nature of cigarettes, greed, and political skullduggery, the truth about smoking tobacco has finally been separated from the lies—and the results are available for mass consumption.

Big tobacco has traditionally been able to buy plenty of friends and influence people in Congress with hefty campaign contributions and aggressive lobbying. During the 1995–96 election cycle, for example, Philip Morris gave more than $4.2

million in campaign contributions, making it the single largest donor in the country. Overall, the industry contributed $10.3 million in 1995-96. It is next to impossible for politicians on the tobacco dole to vote for the health of our youth and the rest of the population when those same politicians are receiving large amounts of money to vote against tobacco taxes and reform. The tobacco industry is making a tremendous amount of money from smokers so they can easily afford to give the money to those who can help them in their fight. They have also used large sums of money to blast us all with propaganda on radio, television, and in print.

My "favorite" tobacco industry ad spewed out the following skewed logic. The ad tugs on our emotions, saying we should not increase taxes on cigarettes because the tax will have the greatest impact on those individuals who have an annual income of less than $30,000—implying that the fiscally "downtrodden" are once again carrying yet another unfair tax burden. If we accept that the population doing most of the smoking is, in fact, this income group, it seems to me they should not be burning their money for cigarettes. While we all have to pay income tax and sales taxes, the tobacco tax is one that no one has to pay. Just don't buy cigarettes. No cigarettes—no taxes! Simple? Sure, there would be no problem if cigarettes were not addictive as tobacco executives would have us believe. Such tobacco industry cover-ups would soon change. Read on.

Tobacco costs to our society are best measured by the number of people who die or suffer illness because of its use, and lost productivity. In 1990, lost economic productivity caused by smoking cost the U.S. economy $47.2 billion, according to the Office of Technology Assessment. Adjusted for inflation, the total economic cost of smoking is now more than $100 billion per year. This does not include costs associated with diseases caused by environmental tobacco smoke (ETS), burn care resulting from cigarette smoking-related fires, or perinatal care for low-birthweight infants of mothers who smoke. Health care expenditures caused directly by smoking totaled $50 billion in 1993, according to the Centers for Disease Control and Prevention. Forty-three percent of these costs were paid by government funds, including Medicaid and Medicare. Tobacco costs Medicare more than $10 billion per year. Smoking alone costs Medicaid $12.9 billion per year—about one-seventh of the total Medicaid budget.

The impact of cigarette smoking on state Medicaid budgets varies among states, ranging from $1.9 billion in New York to $11.4 million in Wyoming. Recently, states have sued the tobacco industry seeking reimbursement for billions of dollars the state had spent on smoking-related illnesses. In 1996, my own state of Texas filed a lawsuit against the tobacco industry. Two years later the industry settled the lawsuit with Texas for $17.3 billion.

Even though smokers die younger than the average American, over the course of their lives, current and former smokers generate an estimated $501 billion in excess health care costs. On average, each cigarette pack sold costs Americans more than $3.90 in smoking-related expenses.

With all the information readily available on the insidious disaster of smoking these days, it continues to amaze me that anyone decides to start. I'm no Pollyanna, nor holier than thou about smoking addiction. Having been a smoker, I know firsthand how difficult it is to stop. Anyone who is currently smoking is addicted or they would quit—unless, of course, they have a death wish. Smokers who claim they can quit any time they please and that they just "like to smoke" are lying to themselves. I know. I remember the death grip cigarettes had on me. I won't ever forget how my body craved them as I went through withdrawal. The urge to light up was intense. People are addicted, so they say they don't want to stop. Why would anyone, of their own free will, choose to spend nearly $4 per pack for a dirty, nasty, addictive, hazardous habit that simply burns up?

On October 13, 1999, the inevitable finally occurred. After years of dodging the facts and denying the health hazards of cigarette smoking, tobacco giant Philip Morris acknowledged that cigarette smoking causes lung cancer and other diseases. A series of public statements appeared in the media and on a new company Web site launched as part of a lavish image-building campaign for the world's biggest cigarette maker. Philip Morris addressed health issues for smokers with two major announcements on their Web site.

1. *Cigarette Smoking and Disease in Smokers:* There is an overwhelming medical and scientific consensus that cigarette smoking causes lung cancer, heart disease, emphysema and other serious diseases in smokers. Smokers are far more likely to develop serious diseases, like lung cancer, than non-smokers. There is no "safe" cigarette. These are and have been the messages of public health authorities worldwide. Smokers and potential smokers should rely on these messages in making all smoking-related decisions.
2. *Cigarette Smoking and Addiction:* Cigarette smoking is addictive, as that term is most commonly used today. It can be very difficult to quit smoking, but this should not deter smokers who want to quit from trying to do so.

I hope this public admission by the tobacco giant has a marked impact on the reduction of cigarette smoking and the health hazards it causes. From this point onward, the consumer is now fully briefed. A new era of health conscious citizens is doable and well within our grasp. Time will tell how smart we are as a society.

My Own Backyard

I am pleased to say that I have been influential in getting several restaurants in my local community to become completely nonsmoking. I'm a frequent patron of The Cactus Flower Restaurant in Fort Worth, Texas. Although the restaurant had separate smoking and nonsmoking sections, the nonsmoking section was always full while the smoking section had many empty tables. But smokers did come and they would often flock to the bathrooms, which had not been designated nonsmoking areas. Patrons would often smoke in the checkout line as well—which was against the law.

My mission was clear. I began complaining to the restaurant owner that I was unable to use the smoke-filled restroom. I also informed him that it was against the law to allow anyone to smoke in the checkout line. At first, the owner told me he didn't want to offend customers by telling them they couldn't smoke in line. He needed a verbal cranial adjustment. I calmly explained he was offending me, one of his loyal nonsmoking customers. Was I somehow less important? He hadn't considered that perspective. From then on, no one was allowed to smoke in the line or in the restroom. I persisted. Every time I saw Phil Greer, owner of the restaurant, I would nag him about the smoking issue. Like many in the restaurant business, Phil believed he would lose business if he converted to all nonsmoking, which couldn't have been further from the truth.

In 1990, San Luis Obispo, California, became the nation's first community to ban all public indoor smoking. Nonsmokers have the right to go to any bar or restaurant in town and not be assaulted by noxious fumes. Enforcement problems are nonexistent. Tourists love the smoke-free environment and the local bar and restaurant trade is booming. The numbers tell the story. There are three times as many nonsmokers in the U.S. as smokers. Because they hate smoke, many nonsmokers avoid bars and restaurants that allow smoking. These establishments are making a foolish business decision because, without a doubt, they are losing revenue.

One fine morning when I came to The Cactus Flower for breakfast, there was a sign prominently displayed on the front door. The announcement proclaimed that the restaurant would be entirely nonsmoking beginning January, 1997. Yes! Hear Ye, Hear Ye. This was a breakthrough and great news to me and, as it turned out, a smart decision for Phil. Shortly after the conversion to all nonsmoking, he let me know that his business had never been better. I didn't have to say I told you so. In all the years since Phil put an end to folks lighting up, his business has continued to thrive in a healthy environment. The former overflow of nonsmoking patrons could now be accommodated at tables formerly reserved for smokers. Now, he has people waiting to get in and no empty tables as before. I call that a win-win situation. An unexpected bonus was that smokers didn't stop coming back either. The food was very good. A neighboring city, Arlington, Texas, also passed an ordinance prohibiting smoking in its restaurants. Since I've made it my business to patronize only nonsmoking establishments, I'll often "go the extra mile" and drive there for dinner. Money talks. The momentum is catching.

In 1999, the American Lung Association reported that Maine joined a small list of states prohibiting smoking in restaurants. The law, which authorizes $100 fines for restaurateurs or patrons who violate the ban, makes exceptions for stand-alone bars. Vermont and Utah have similar laws, and California prohibits smoking in bars as well as restaurants. A number of cities across the nation also have imposed smoking bans in restaurants. There are also restaurants in every state that aren't waiting for politics—they're going nonsmoking on their own initiative because it's a smart business move.

Starting in January 2000, all restaurants in Fort Worth were to be exclusively nonsmoking, except those that provide a separate ventilation system. Unfortunately I have found that the ventilation systems are not adequate to prevent smoke from interfering with my meal. The tobacco industry has brainwashed many in the restaurant business, convincing them that patronage will drop off if they change to all smoke-free. We know this is not the case. In most situations, revenues actually increase when an establishment goes nonsmoking. Many smokers have gotten used to the idea that others don't want to inhale their habit and that they can't smoke whenever and wherever they wish—which admittedly is stressful when you're addicted.

WEB SITES

Action on Smoking and Health:
A national legal-action antismoking organization entirely supported by tax-deductible contributions
http://ash.org/

American Cancer Society
http://www.cancer.org/

American Lung Association
http://www.lungusa.org/

Ask Dr. Andrew Weil - Health & Wellness
www.pathfinder.com/drweil/

The Block Center
Information about products available to assist parents in helping their children with health and learning
www.blockcenter.com

Cancer Care, Inc.
Dedicated to providing emotional support, information, and practical help to people with cancer and their loved ones
http://www.cancercare.org/

Clinical Pearls News: Monthly summaries on 100 to 200 health related articles
http://www.clinicalpearls.com/

Common Cause
Citizens working to end special-interest politics and reform government ethics
http://commoncause.org/

Diagnostic Web
Information on diagnostic imaging procedures, written for the public
http://diagnosticweb.com/public.htm

The Hemlock Society
Oldest and largest right-to-die organization in the United States
http://www.hemlock.org/

Opensecrets
Online Source for Money in Politics Data
http://www.opensecrets.org/home/index.asp

The Osteopathic Home Page
http://www.osteohome.com/

Spectrum: The Wholistic News Magazine
http://www.spectrumlink.com/intro.htm

BIBLIOGRAPHY

Nutritional Modulation of Behavior and Immunocompetence, John E. Morley, MB, *Nutrition Reviews*, August 1994; 52(8): S6–S8.

Nutrition: Review of 1994, Robert M. Russell, M.D., *JAMA*, June 7, 1995; 273(21):1699–1700.

Antioxidant Vitamins and Cancer, Charles H. Hennekens, M.D., *The American Journal of Medicine*, September 6, 1994: 97(Suppl 3A):3A–2S–2A–4S.

Protective Effects of Raw Vegetables and Fruit Against Lung Cancer Among Smokers and Ex-Smokers: A Case-Control Study in the Tokai Area of Japan, Chang-ming Gao, et al. *Japanese Journal of Cancer Research*, June 1993; 84:594–600.

Micronutrients and Cancer Risk, Walter C. Willett, *American Journal of Clinical Nutrition*, 1994:59(Suppl.)1162S–65S.

Phytochemicals: Plants Against Cancer, David Schardt, *Nutritional Action Health Letter*, April 1994; 21(3):7–13.

What are People Dying of on High Air Pollution Days?, Joel Schwartz, *Environmental Research*, 1994; 64:26–35.

Radon and Man-Made Vitreous Fibers, James E. Lockey, M.D., MS and Ross, Clara Sue, M.D., JD, *Journal of Allergy and Clinical Immunology*, August 1994; 94(2)/Part 2:310–317.

Experimental Study of the Therapeutic Effect of Folate, Vitamin A, and Vitamin B_{12} on Squamous Metaplasia of the Bronchial Epithelium, Tamiko Kamei, M.D. et al. *Cancer* April 15, 1993:71(8):2477–83.

Mighty Vitamins: The One-A-Day Wonders Bidding to Outstrip Their Roles as Supplements, P.J. Skerrett, *Medical World News*, January 1993; 24–32.

Antioxidants and Cancer, Bonnie Liebman, *Nutrition Action Health Letter*, July/August 1992; 1,5–7.

Cigarette Smoking and Cervical Cancer, Harriet O. Smith, M.D. et al. *The Female Patient*, October 1992; 17:48–60.

Fruit, Vegetables, and Cancer Prevention: A Review of the Epidemiologic Evidence, Gladys Block, M.D., et al. *Nutrition and Cancer*, 1992; 18:1–29.

Vegetables, Fruit and Cancer I: Epidemiology, Kristi A. Steinmetz,. and John D. Potter, *Cancer Causes and Control*, 1991; 2:325–357.

Vegetables, Fruits and Cancer II: Mechanisms, Kristi A. Steinmetz, and John D. Potter, *Cancer Causes and Control*, 1991; 2:427–442.

Garlic, Cauliflower and Soy Sauce Combat Cancer, *Medical Tribune*, September 24, 1992; 34.

Body Mass Index and Lung Cancer Risks, Geoffrey Kabat, and Ernst Winder, *American Journal of Epidemiology*, 1992; 135(7): 769–774.

Dietary Determinates of Lung Cancer: Results From a Case-Controlled Study in Yunnan Province, China, C.A. Swanson, et al. *International Journal of Cancer,* 1992; 50:876–880.

Dietary Factors and the Risk of Lung Cancer: Total Body Evidence, R.B. Shekelle et al. *American Journal of Epidemiology,* September 1, 1991; 134:471–479/*The Journal of Respiratory Diseases,* March 1992; 13(3):390.

High Fat Foods and the Risk of Lung Cancer, Marc T. Goodman et al. *Epidemiology,* July 1992; 3(4):288–299.

Lung Cancer: From Triumph to Tragedy, David T. Carr, *International Journal of Cell Cloning,* 1991; 9:548–558.

Alcohol, Beer and Lung Cancer in Postmenopausal Women: The Iowa Women's Health Study, John D. Potter, M.D., Ph.D. et al. *Annals of Epidemiology,* 1992; 2:587–595.

Nutrition and Cancer: The Gonzalez Study, Robert W. Maver, FSA, MAAA, Vice President and Director of Research, Mutual Benefit of Life, *On the Risk,* 1991; 7(2).

Health Consequences of Smoking—Cancer, Polly A. Newcomb, Ph.D. and Paul P. Carbone, M.D., *Medical Clinics of North America,* March 1992; 76(2):305–331.

Cancer Strides Challenges: Establishment's Therapeutic Claims Overstated, Says Activist Coalition, Bill Ingram, *Medical Tribune,* February 27, 1992; 33(4):1.

Epidemiologic Evidence Regarding Vitamin C and Cancer, Gladys Block, *The American Journal of Clinical Nutrition,* 1991; 54:1310S–14S.

Dietary Vitamin A, Beta-Carotene and Risk of Epidermoid Lung Cancer in Southwestern France, J.F. Dartigues et al. *European Journal of Epidemiology,* 1990; 6(3):261–265.

Intervention Trial in Selenium For The Prevention of Lung Cancer Among Tin Miners in Yunnan, China, Shu-Yu Yu et al. *Biological Trace Element Research*, 1990; 24:105–108.

The Role of Antioxidants in Clinical Practice, A.T. Diplock, Ph.D., *British Journal of Clinical Practice*, July 1990; 44(7):257–258.

Epidemiologic Studies of Antioxidants and Cancer in Humans, Elaine W. Flagg, Ph.D. et al. *Journal of The American College of Nutrition*, 1995; 14(5):419–427.

Beta-Carotene and Cancer: Risk or Protection?, Harri Vainio, *Scandinavian Journal of Work Environmental Health*, 1996; 22(3): 161–163.

Beta-Carotene and Cancer: Where are We Now?, Thomas Edes, M.D., *Journal of the American College of Nutrition*, 1995; 14(3):306–308.

Lifestyle, Environmental Pollution and Lung Cancer in Cities of Liaoning in Northeastern China, Z.-Y. Xu et al. *Lung Cancer* 1996:14(Suppl.1):S149–S160.

Lung Cancer, Regina G. Ziegler, *Cancer Causes and Control*, 1996; 7:157–177.

Low Plasma Cholesterol Predicts an Increased Risk of Lung Cancer in Elderly Women, Andrew K. Chang, B.S. et al. *Preventive Medicine* 1995; 24:557–562.

Tea Consumption and Lung Cancer Risk: A Case-Controlled Study in Okinawa, Japan, Yoshiyuki Ohno et al. *Japanese Journal of Cancer Research*, November, 1995; 86:1027–1034.

Dietary Factors and Lung Cancer Among Men in West Sweden, Gosta Axelsson et al. *International Journal of Epidemiology*, 1996; 25(1):32–39.

Selenium Does not Prevent Nonmelanoma Cancer Recurrence, Elizabeth Mechcatie, *Skin and Allergy News*, June 1996; 4./ Selenium May Reduce the Risk of Colon, Prostate Cancer, Elizabeth Mechcatie, *Family Practice News*, June 1, 1996; 12.

Watercress May Inhibit Smoking-Related Cancer, Sherry Boschert, *Family Practice News*, June 1, 1996; 10.

Vitamins and Cancer: A Practical Means of Prevention?, Karin B. Michels, and Walter C. Willett, *Important Advances in Oncology*, Edited by Vincent P. DeVita et al. 1994; 6:85–114.

The Treatment of Zinc Deficiency Is an Immunotherapy, John W. Hadden, *International Journal of Immunopharmacology*, 1995; 17(9):697–701.

Excess Mortality Among Cigarette Smokers: Changes in 20-Year Interval, Michael J. Thun, M.D., MS et al. *The American Journal of Public Health*, September 1995; 85(9):1223–1230.

The Effects of Beta-Carotene on the Immune System in Cancer, George S. Hughes, *The Nutrition Report*, January 1992; 10(1):1–8.

Beta-Carotene and Vitamin A: Casting Separate Shadows?, Thomas E. Edes, M.D., *The Nutrition Report*, February 1992; 10(2); 9,16.

Plasma Antioxidant Vitamins and Subsequent Cancer Mortality in Twelve-Year Follow-up of the Prospective Basel Study, Hannes B. Stahelin et al. *American Journal of Epidemiology*, 1991; 133:766–75.

Antioxidant Micronutrients and Cancer Prevention, Joanne F. Dorgan, M.P.H., Ph.D., and Arthur Schatzkin, M.D., Dr. P.H., *Hematology/Oncology Clinics of North America*, February 1991; 5(1); 43–68.

Premalignant Lesion: Role of Antioxidant Vitamins Beta-Carotene in Risk Reduction and Prevention of Malignant Transformation, Vishwa N. Singh, and Suzanne K. Gaby, *American Journal of Clinical Nutrition*, 1991; 53:386S–390S.

A Dietary Shield Against Lung Cancer, *Science News*, October 12, 1991; 104:237.

Beta-Carotene and Cancer, H.B. Stahelin, *British Journal of Clinical Practice*, December 1990; 44(11):543–545.

B-Carotene and Cancer Prevention: The Basel Study, Hannes B. Stahelin et al. *American Journal of Clinical Nutrition*, 1991; 53:265S–9S.

Prediagnostic Serum Levels of Carotenoids and Vitamin E as Related to Subsequent Cancer in Washington County, Maryland, George Comstock et al. *American Journal of Clinical Nutrition*, 1991; 53:260S–264S.

A Case-Controlled Study of Dietary Carotene in Men With Lung Cancer and in Men With Other Epithelial Cancers, Ruth W.C. Harris et al. *Nutrition and Cancer*, 1991; 15(1)64–68.

Dietary Antioxidants and The Risk of Lung Cancer, Paul Knekt et al. *The American Journal of Epidemiology*, 1991; 134(5): 417–9.

Lung Cancer and Smoking Trends in The United States Over the Past 25 Years, Lawrence Garfinkle, and Edwin Silverberg, *CA-A Cancer Journal For Clinicians*, May/June1991; 41(3):137–147.

Lung Cancer Kills More Smokers Than Heart Ills, *Medical Tribune*, September 19, 1991; 4.

A Randomized Study Comparing Intermittent to Continuous Administration of Magnesium Aspartate Hydrochloride in

Cisplatin-Induced Hypomagnesemia, E.E. Vokes et al. *British Journal of Cancer*, 1990; 62:1015–1017.

Vitamin C and Cancer Prevention: The Epidemiologic Evidence, Gladys Block, *American Journal of Clinical Nutrition*, 1991; 53:270I–282S.

Fibrinogen Levels From Passive Smoke, *Medical Tribune*, September 19, 1991; 10.

Harmful Effects of Passive Smoke, Susan B. Meltzer, MPH, and Eli Meltzer, M.D., *Western Journal of Medicine*, April 1991; 154(4):457–458.

Lung Cancer and Exposure to Tobacco Smoke in the Household, Dwight T. Janerich, DDS, M.P.H. et al. *New England Journal of Medicine*, September 6, 1990; 323(10):632–636.

Concurrent Cisplatin and Etoposide with Radiotherapy in Locally Advanced Non-Small Cell Lung Cancer, G.G. Friess, M. Baikadi, W.H. Harvey, *Cancer Treatment Reports*, July-August 1987; 71(7-8):681–4.

Selenium In The Diet, Margaret P. Rayman, D.Phil., *Clinical Pearls News*, July 1997, Vol.7, No.7.

Effects of Aerobic Exercise on the Physical Performance and Incidence of Treatment-Related Complications After High-Dose Chemotherapy, Fernando Dimeo et al. *Blood*, November 1, 1997; 90(9):3390–3394.

The Protective Role of Selenium on the Toxicity of Cisplatin-Contained Chemotherapy Regimen in Cancer Patients, Ya-Jun Hu et al. *Biological Trace Elements Research*, 1997; 56:331–341.

Phyto-Oestrogens and Western Disease, Herman Adlercreutz, and Witold Mazur, *Annals of Medicine*, 1997; 29:95–120.

Experimental and Epidemiological Evidence of the Cancer-Preventive Effects of Panax ginseng C.A. Meyer, Taik-Koo Yun, M.D., *Nutrition Reviews*, November, 1996; 54(11):S71–S81.

Decline on Serum Total Cholesterol and the Risk of Death From Cancer, Mahmoud Zureik et al. *Epidemiology*, March, 1997; 8(2):137–143.

Supplemental Ascorbate in the Supportive Treatment of Cancer: Prolongation of Survival Times in Terminal Human Cancer, Ewan Cameron, and Linus Pauling, *Proceedings of the National Academy of Sciences*, U.S.A., October, 1976; 73(10): 3685–3689.

Vitamin Trials and Cancer, Carmen Wheatley, *The Lancet*, June 21, 1997; 349:1844–1845.

Dietary Omega-3 Polyunsaturated Fatty Acids Plus Vitamin E Restore Immunodeficiency and Prolong Survival for Severely Ill Patients With Generalized Malignancy, Charalambos A. Gogos, M.D. et al. *Cancer*, January 15, 1998; 82(2):395–402.

RECOMMENDED READING

Cousins, Norman. *Anatomy of an Illness: As Perceived by the Patient*. New York: Bantam Doubleday, 1991.

Peale, Norman Vincent. *The Power of Positive Thinking*. New York: Ballantine Books, 1996.

Siegel, Bernie. *Love, Medicine and Miracles*. New York: Harper/Perennial Library, 1990.

Simonton, Carl, Stephanie Matthews-Simonton and James L. Creighton. *Getting Well Again*. New York: Bantam, 1992.

Taylor, Nadine. *Green Tea*. Kensington Publishing, 1998.

Weil, Andrew. *Natural Health, Natural Medicine*. New York: Houghton Mifflin, 1998.

Weil, Andrew. *Spontaneous Healing*. New York: Ballantine Books, 1996.

Werbach, Melvyn. *Nutritional Influences on Illness*. New Canaan, CT: Keats Publishing, 1996.

PUBLISHER'S RESOURCE GUIDE

Distributors of Nutritional Supplements:

Products of Nature
1-800-770-7039
www.prodnature.com

MegaFood
1-800-848-2542
www.megafood.com

Carlson® Laboratories
1-800-323-4141
www.carlsonlabs.com

Source Naturals®
1-800-815-2333
www.sourcenaturals.com

Jarrow Formulas™
1-800-726-0886
www.jarrow.com

Tree of Life®
www.treeoflife.com

Martek-DHA
1-888-658-7246
www.martekbio.com

Wakunaga of America-Garlic
1-800-421-2998
www.kyolic.com

Catalog Company (Mail Order):

N.E.E.D.S.
1-800-634-1380
www.needs.com

An excellent resource for top-notch environmental products and supplements. They carry a full line of air filters, water filters and purifiers, natural household cleansers, and other products.

Natural Food Companies:

Cheese—Organic

Country Hills Organic, Inc.
330-893-2596

Pure Pastures Organic Cheese
A complete family of organic cheeses, available in six traditional styles, including Cheddar, Colby, Swiss and Havarti, as well as an assortment of yogurt cheeses.

Noni Juice

Tahiti Traders
1-888-766-1234
www.tahititraders.com

The noni plant contains naturally occurring vitamins, minerals, elements, enzymes, beneficial alkaloids, co-factors, plant sterols, antioxidants, phytonutrients, and bioflavonoids.

Nuts, Nut Butters and Seeds—Organic

Living Tree Community Foods
1-800-260-5534
www.livingtreecommunity.com

Organically grown nuts and nut butters, including almonds (many varieties), macadamia nuts, pine nuts, pumpkin seeds, sunflower seeds, walnut quarters, raw almond butter, and raw cashew butter. They refrigerate their nuts, seeds and nut butters until the day they are shipped.

Oils

Available from the following companies:

Omega Nutrition
Essential Balance Jr.

Omega's proprietary blend of five fresh-pressed oils, scientifically blended in the evolutionary 1:1 omega-3/omega-6 ratio. Contains certified organic flax, sunflower, sesame, pumpkin and borage oils. Also contains gamma-linolenic acid (GLA) and omega-6 fatty acids.

Flax Seed Oil

Unrefined and certified organic, grown without pesticides or artificial fertilizers and processed using Omega's exclusive omegaflo® process.

Olive Oil

Made from unrefined, extra-virgin olives that are fresh-pressed and omegaflo® bottled.

Tree of Life®

Tree of Life High Lignan Flax Oil

Contains all the antioxidants of their original Organic Flax Oil plus the added benefits of high fiber lignans. Bottled in liquid form. Available in health food stores.

Tree of Life Organic Extra Virgin Olive Oil

Bella Via Organic Extra Virgin Olive Oil

Made from the first pressing of 100% organic olives imported from the Andalusia region of Spain.

Poultry

Sheltons Poultry, Inc.
1-800-541-1833

Free-range chicken and turkey with no added antibiotics. Available in natural foods stores. Noted health expert, Andrew Weil, M.D., cautions people to avoid eating poultry and meat with added antibiotics, which the Centers for Disease Control has linked to drug-resistant strains of disease-causing bacteria.

Seafood

Capilano Pacific
1-877-391-WILD (9453)
www.capilanopacific.com
Wildfish™

This company is a source for wild-caught salmon. Most of the salmon available in restaurants and stores are farm-raised. Usually this means medications such as antibiotics have been added to the feed, as well as synthetic coloring. Wild-caught salmon has none of these problems and a high level of omega-3 fatty acids and much less fat than farm-raised salmon. It tastes better as well. Also available: halibut, tuna and lox without any added chemicals.

Teas (Green)

Available from the following companies:

Great Eastern Sun
1-800-334-5809
www.great-eastern-sun.com

Haiku® Organic Japanese Teas

Organic Original Sencha Green Tea: the finest grade of green leaf tea available, made from the tender young leaves of selected tea bushes, cut at the peak of their flavor, rolled, steamed, and briefly dried. Contains 100% Nagata Japanese Organic Sencha Green Tea Leaves and Buds. Available in tea bags and bulk.

Organic Original Hojicha Roasted Green Tea: lower in caffeine than Sencha, Hojicha has a subtle smoky and rich flavor that is quite different from that of Sencha. Contains 100% Nagata Japanese Organic Hojicha Roasted Green Tea Leaves and Stems. Available in tea bags and bulk.

Triple Leaf Tea, Inc.
1-800-552-7448
www.tripleleaf-tea.com

Authentic traditional Chinese medicinal teas in tea bags, including different varieties of green tea. Triple Leaf has a natural method of using a natural carbon dioxide decaffeinating process that maintains almost all of the green tea's beneficial antioxidants.

Tea—Ginger

Triple Leaf Tea, Inc.
1-800-552-7448
www.tripleleaf-tea.com
Made from 100% ginger root. Available in tea bags.

Tree of Life®
www.treeoflife.com
There are many fine health food stores all over the country that carry top-notch products. Many stores are supplied by an excellent company known as Tree of Life, a distributor of high qual-

ity natural foods at moderate prices. When shopping at health food stores, you can ask for Tree of Life products. If a store doesn't carry a particular product, they can order it for you.

Tree of Life Frozen Organic Vegetables
Certified organically grown.
Broccoli
Corn
Green Peas
Spinach

Tree of Life Frozen Organic Fruit
Loaded with nutrients without any added chemicals. They are often difficult to obtain.
Strawberries
Blueberries
Raspberries

Tree of Life Frozen Smoothie Makers
Fresh-frozen chunks of 100% organic fruit. Ideal for juicing.
Banana, Rasberry, Strawberry

Tree of Life Pasta Sauce
Original and Salt-Free—in glass jars.
This organic pasta sauce is made from vine-ripened, specially selected premium tomatoes that are grown for their sweetness and flavor.

Tree of Life Organic Tamari and Shoyu
Made from organic soybeans and wheat. Excellent for steamed vegetables and fish.
Shoyu
Wheat-Free Tamari

Harmony Farms Light Soymilk
Made from certified GMO-free soybeans. Available in orange or vanilla flavors, enriched with extra vitamins and minerals.

Harmony Farms Soy Burgers
High in protein and isoflavones. Available in the following flavors: original, garlic, mushroom and onion.

Tree of Life Tofu
Third party certified organic tofu. Available in fourteen delicious varieties, including 30% reduced fat tofu, organic baked tofu, organic oriental baked tofu, and organic island spice baked tofu.

Tree of Life Advantage\10™ Entrees
These products are all natural, vegetarian, cholesterol-free, and with less than 10% of their calories derived from fat.

Advantage\10™ Soups: Packed in single serving bowls. Cajun Black Bean, Southwestern Chili, and Tuscan Vegetable Minestrone.

Advantage\10™ Veggie Burgers: Southwestern Vegetable Burger and Mushroom Burger.

Advantage\10™ Fruit Smoothies: A non-dairy blend of soy milk, fruit, and whole grains. Raspberry, Strawberry, and Strawberry-Banana.

Tree of Life Creamy Cashew Butter

Tree of Life Organic Sesame Tahini

Tree of Life Organic Almond Butter—Creamy or Crunchy